The Art of Capacity Planning

Other resources from O'Reilly

The Art of Capacity Planning

John Allspaw

O'REILLY®

Beijing • Cambridge • Farnham • Köln • Sebastopol • Taipei • Tokyo

The Art of Capacity Planning
by John Allspaw

Copyright © 2008 Yahoo! Inc. All rights reserved. Printed in the United States of America.

Published by O'Reilly Media, Inc. 1005 Gravenstein Highway North, Sebastopol, CA 95472

O'Reilly books may be purchased for educational, business, or sales promotional use. Online editions are also available for most titles (*safari.oreilly.com*). For more information, contact our corporate/institutional sales department: (800) 998-9938 or *corporate@oreilly.com*.

Editor: Andy Oram

Production Editor: Rachel Monaghan

Production Services: Octal Publishing, Inc.

Indexer: Angela Howard

Cover Designer: Mark Paglietti

Interior Designer: Marcia Friedman

Illustrator: Robert Romano

Printing History:

September 2008: First Edition.

 This book uses RepKover™, a durable and flexible lay-flat binding.

ISBN: 978-0-596-51857-8

[M]

To my father, James W. Allspaw, who taught me that
engineering is about getting things done, not just thinking things up.

CONTENTS

Preface

SOMEWHERE AROUND 3 A.M. ON JULY 7TH, 2005, MY COWORKER, CAL HENDERSON, AND I WERE FINISHING up some final details before moving all of the traffic for our website, Flickr.com, to its new home: a Yahoo! data center in Texas. The original infrastructure in Vancouver was becoming more and more overloaded, and suffering from serious power and space constraints. Since Yahoo! had just acquired Flickr, it was time to bring new capacity online. It was about an hour after we changed DNS records to point to our shiny new servers that Cal happened to glance at the news. The London subway had just been bombed.

Londoners responded with their camera phones, among other things. Over the next 24 hours, Flickr saw more traffic than ever before, as photos from the disaster were uploaded to the site. News outlets began linking to the photos, and traffic on our new servers went through the roof.

It was not only a great example of citizen journalism, but also an object lesson—sadly, one born of tragedy—in capacity planning. Traffic can be sporadic and unpredictable at times. Had we not moved over to the new data center, Flickr.com wouldn't have been available that day.

Capacity planning has been around since ancient times, with roots in everything from economics to engineering. In a basic sense, capacity planning is resource management. When resources are finite, and come at a cost, you need to do some capacity planning.

When a civil engineering firm designs a new highway system, it's planning for capacity, as is a power company planning to deliver electricity to a metropolitan area. In some ways, their concerns have a lot in common with web operations; many of the basic concepts and concerns can be applied to all three disciplines.

While systems administration has been around since the 1960s, the branch focused on serving websites is still emerging. A large part of web operations is capacity planning and management. Those are *processes*, not *tasks*, and they are composed of many different parts. Although every organization goes about it differently, the basic concepts are the same:

- Ensure proper resources (servers, storage, network, etc.) are available to handle expected and unexpected loads.

- Have a clearly defined procurement and approval system in place.

- Be prepared to justify capital expenditures in support of the business.

- Have a deployment and management system in place to manage the resources once they are deployed.

Why I Wrote This Book

One of my frustrations as an operations engineering manager was not having somewhere to turn to help me figure out how much equipment we'd need to keep running. Existing books on the topic of computer capacity planning were focused on the mathematical *theory* of resource planning, rather than the practical *implementation* of the whole process.

A lot of literature addressed only rudimentary models of website use cases, and lacked specific information or advice. Instead, they tended to offer mathematical models designed to illustrate the principles of queuing theory, which is the foundation of traditional capacity planning. This approach might be mathematically interesting and elegant, but it doesn't help the operations engineer when informed he has a week to prepare for some unknown amount of additional traffic—perhaps due to the launch of a super new feature—or seeing his site dying under the weight of a link from the front page of Yahoo!, Digg, or CNN.

I've found most books on web capacity planning were written with the implied assumption that concepts and processes found in non-web environments, such as manufacturing or industrial engineering, applied uniformly to website environments as well. While some of the theory surrounding such planning may indeed be similar, the practical application of those concepts doesn't map very well to the short timelines of website development.

In most web development settings, it's been my observation that change happens too fast and too often to allow for the detailed and rigorous capacity investigations common to other fields. By the time the operations engineer comes up with the queuing model for his system, new code is deployed and the usage characteristics have likely already changed dramatically. Or some other technological, social, or real-world event occurs, making all of the modeling and simulations irrelevant.

What I've found to be far more helpful, is talking to colleagues in the industry—people who come up against many of the same scaling and capacity issues. Over time, I've had contact with many different companies, each employing diverse architectures, and each experiencing different problems. But quite often they shared very similar approaches to solutions. My hope is that I can illustrate some of these approaches in this book.

Focus and Topics

This book is not about building complex models and simulations, nor is it about spending time running benchmarks over and over. It's not about mathematical concepts such as Little's Law, Markov chains, or Poisson arrival rates.

What this book is about is *practical* capacity planning and management that can take place in the real world. It's about using real tools, and being able to adapt to changing usage on a website that will (hopefully) grow over time. When you have a flat tire on the highway, you could spend a lot of time trying to figure out the cause, or you can get on with the obvious task of installing the spare and getting back on the road.

This is the approach I'm presenting to capacity planning: adaptive, not theoretical.

Keep in mind a good deal of the information in this book will seem a lot like common sense—this is a good thing. Quite often the simplest approaches to problem solving are the best ones, and capacity planning is no exception.

This book will cover the process of capacity planning for growing websites, including measurement, procurement, and deployment. I'll discuss some of the more popular and proven measurement tools and techniques. Most of these tools run in both LAMP and Windows-based environments. As such, I'll try to keep the discussion as platform-agnostic as possible.

Of course, it's beyond the scope of this book to cover the details of every database, web server, caching server, and storage solution. Instead, I'll use examples of each to illustrate the process and concepts, but this book is not meant to be an implementation guide. The intention is to be as generic as possible when it comes to explaining resource management—it's the process itself we want to emphasize.

For example, a database is used to store data and provide responses to queries. Most of the more popular databases allow for replicating data to other servers, which enhances redundancy, performance, and architectural decisions. It also assists the technical implementation of replication with Postgres, Oracle, or MySQL (a topic for other books). This book covers what replication means in terms of planning capacity and deployment.

Essentially, this book is about measuring, planning, and managing growth for a web application, regardless of the underlying technologies you choose.

Audience for This Book

This book is for systems, storage, database, and network administrators, engineering managers, and of course, capacity planners.

It's intended for anyone who hopes (or perhaps fears) their website will grow like those of Facebook, Flickr, MySpace, Twitter, and others—companies that underwent the trial-by-fire process of scaling up as their usage skyrocketed. The approaches in this text come from real experience with sites where traffic has grown both heavily and rapidly. If you expect the popularity of your site will dramatically increase the amount of traffic you experience, then please read this book.

Organization of the Material

Chapter 1, *Goals, Issues, and Processes in Capacity Planning*, presents the issues that arise over and over on heavily trafficked websites.

Chapter 2, *Setting Goals for Capacity*, illustrates the various concerns involved with planning for the growth of a web application, and how capacity fits into the overall picture of availability and performance.

Chapter 3, *Measurement: Units of Capacity*, discusses capacity measurement and monitoring.

Chapter 4, *Predicting Trends*, explains how to turn measurement data into forecasts, and how trending fits into the overall planning process.

Chapter 5, *Deployment*, discusses concepts related to deployment; automation of installation, configuration, and management.

Appendix A, *Virtualization and Cloud Computing*, discusses where virtualization and cloud services fit into a capacity plan.

Appendix B, *Dealing with Instantaneous Growth*, offers insight into what can be done in capacity crisis situations, and some best practices for dealing with site outages.

Appendix C, *Capacity Tools*, is an annotated list of measurement, installation, configuration, and management tools highlighted throughout the book.

Conventions Used in This Book

The following typographical conventions are used in this book:

Italic
> Indicates new terms, URLs, filenames, Unix utilities, and command-line options.

`Constant width`
> Indicates the contents of files, the output from commands, and generally anything found in programs.

Constant width bold

> Shows commands or other text that should be typed literally by the user, and parts of code or files highlighted to stand out for discussion.

Constant width italic

> Shows text that should be replaced with user-supplied values.

Using Code Examples

This book is here to help you get your job done. In general, you may use the code in this book in your programs and documentation. You do not need to contact us for permission unless you're reproducing a significant portion of the code. For example, writing a program that uses several chunks of code from this book does not require permission. Selling or distributing a CD-ROM of examples from O'Reilly books *does* require permission. Answering a question by citing this book and quoting example code does not require permission. Incorporating a significant amount of example code from this book into your product's documentation *does* require permission.

We appreciate, but do not require, attribution. An attribution usually includes the title, author, publisher, and ISBN. For example: *"The Art of Capacity Planning* by John Allspaw. Copyright 2008 Yahoo! Inc., 978-0-596-51857-8."

If you feel your use of code examples falls outside fair use or the permission given above, feel free to contact us at *permissions@oreilly.com*.

We'd Like to Hear from You

Please address comments and questions concerning this book to the publisher:

> O'Reilly Media, Inc.
> 1005 Gravenstein Highway North
> Sebastopol, CA 95472
> 800-998-9938 (in the United States or Canada)
> 707-829-0515 (international or local)
> 707-829-0104 (fax)

We have a web page for this book, where we list errata, examples, and any additional information. You can access this page at:

> *http://www.oreilly.com/catalog/9780596518578*

To comment or ask technical questions about this book, send email to:

> *bookquestions@oreilly.com*

For more information about our books, conferences, Resource Centers, and the O'Reilly Network, see our website at:

> *http://www.oreilly.com*

Safari® Books Online

 When you see a Safari® Books Online icon on the cover of your favorite technology book, that means the book is available online through the O'Reilly Network Safari Bookshelf.

Safari offers a solution that's better than e-books. It's a virtual library that lets you easily search thousands of top tech books, cut and paste code samples, download chapters, and find quick answers when you need the most accurate, current information. Try it for free at *http://safari.oreilly.com*.

Acknowledgments

It's simply not possible to thank everyone enough in this single, small paragraph, but I will most certainly mention their names. Most of the material in this book was derived from experiences in the trenches, and there are many people who have toughed it out in those trenches alongside me. Peter Norby, Gil Raphaelli, Kevin Collins, Dathan Pattishall, Cal Henderson, Aaron Cope, Paul Hammond, Paul Lloyd, Serguei Mourachov and Chad Dickerson need special thanks, as does Heather Champ and the entire Flickr customer care team. Thank you Flickr development engineering: you all think like operations engineers and for that I am grateful. Thanks to Stewart Butterfield and Caterina Fake for convincing me to join the Flickr team early on. Thanks to David Filo and Hugo Gunnarsen for forcing me to back up my hardware requests with real data. Major thanks go out to Kevin Murphy for providing so much material in the automated deployment chapter. Thanks to Andy Oram and Isabel Kunkle for editing, and special thanks to my good friend Chris Colin for excellent pre-pre-editing advice.

Thanks to Adam Jacob, Matt St. Onge, Jeremy Zawodny, and Theo Schlossnagle for the super tech review.

Much thanks to Matt Mullenweg and Don MacAskill for sharing their cloud infrastructure use cases.

Most important, thanks to my wife, Elizabeth Kairys, for encouraging and supporting me in this insane endeavor. Accomplishing this without her would have been impossible.

CHAPTER ONE

Goals, Issues, and Processes in Capacity Planning

THIS CHAPTER IS DESIGNED TO HELP YOU ASSEMBLE AND USE THE WEALTH OF TOOLS AND TECHNIQUES presented in the following chapters. If you do not grasp the concepts introduced in this chapter, reading the remainder of this book will be like setting out on the open ocean without knowing how to use a compass, sextant, or GPS device—you can go around in circles forever.

When you break them down, capacity planning and management—the steps taken to organize the resources your site needs to run properly—are, in fact, simple processes. You begin by asking the question: what performance do you need from your website?

First, define the application's overall load and capacity requirements using *specific* metrics, such as response times, consumable capacity, and peak-driven processing. Peak-driven processing is the workload experienced by your application's resources (web servers, databases, etc.) during peak usage. The process, illustrated in Figure 1-1, involves answering these questions:

1. How well is the current infrastructure working?

   Measure the characteristics of the workload for each piece of the architecture that comprises your applications—web server, database server, network, and so on—and compare them to what you came up with for your performance requirements mentioned above.

2. What do you need in the future to maintain acceptable performance?

   Predict the future based on what you know about past system performance then marry that prediction with what you can afford, and a realistic timeline. Determine what you'll need and *when* you'll need it.

3. How can you install and manage resources after you gather what you need?

   Deploy this new capacity with industry-proven tools and techniques.

4. Rinse, repeat.

   Iterate and calibrate your capacity plan over time.

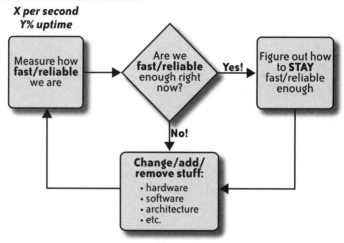

FIGURE 1-1. The process for determining the capacity you need

Your ultimate goal lies between not buying enough hardware and wasting your money on too much hardware.

Let's suppose you're a supermarket manager. One of your tasks is to manage the schedule of cashiers. Your challenge is picking the right number of cashiers working at any moment. Assign too few, and the checkout lines will become long, and the customers irate. Schedule too many working at once, and you're spending more money than necessary. The trick is finding the right balance.

Now, think of the cashiers as servers, and the customers as client browsers. Be aware some cashiers might be better than others, and each day might bring a different amount of customers. Then you need to take into consideration your supermarket is getting more and more popular. A seasoned supermarket manager intuitively knows these variables exist, and attempts to strike a good balance between not frustrating the customers and not paying too many cashiers.

Welcome to the supermarket of web operations.

Quick and Dirty Math

The ideas I've just presented are hardly new, innovative, or complex. Engineering disciplines have always employed back-of-the-envelope calculations; the field of web operations is no different.

Because we're looking to make judgments and predictions on a quickly changing landscape, approximations will be necessary, and it's important to realize what that means in terms of limitations in the process. Being aware of when detail is needed and when it's not is crucial to forecasting budgets and cost models. Unnecessary detail means wasted time. Lacking the proper detail can be fatal.

Predicting When Your Systems Will Fail

Knowing when each piece of your infrastructure will fail (gracefully or not) is crucial to capacity planning. Capacity planning for the web, more often than one would like to admit, looks like the approach shown in Figure 1-2.

FIGURE 1-2. Finding failure points

Including this information as part of your calculations is mandatory, not optional. However, determining the limits of each portion of your site's backend can be tricky. An easily segmented architecture helps you find the limits of your current hardware configurations. You can then use those capacity ceilings as a basis for predicting future growth.

For example, let's assume you have a database server that responds to queries from your frontend web servers. Planning for capacity means knowing the answers to questions such as these:

- Taking into account the specific hardware configuration, how many queries per second (QPS) can the database server manage?
- How many QPS can it serve before performance degradation affects end user experience?

Adjusting for periodic spikes and subtracting some comfortable percentage of headroom (or safety factor, which we'll talk about later) will render a single number with which you can characterize that database configuration vis-à-vis the specific role. Once you find that "red line" metric, you'll know:

- The load that will cause the database to fail, which will allow you to set alert thresholds accordingly.

- What to expect from adding (or removing) similar database servers to the backend.

- When to start sizing another order of new database capacity.

We'll talk more about these last points in the coming chapters. One thing to note is the entire capacity planning process is going to be architecture-specific. This means the calculations you make to predict increasing capacity may have other constraints specific to your particular application.

For example, to spread out the load, a LAMP application might utilize a MySQL server as a master database in which all live data is written and maintained, and use a second, replicated slave database for read-only database operations. Adding more slave databases to scale the read-only traffic is generally an appropriate technique, but many large websites (including Flickr) have been forthright about their experiences with this approach, and the limits they've encountered. There is a limit to how many read-only slave databases you can add before you begin to see diminishing returns as the rate and volume of changes to data on the master database may be more than the replicated slaves can sustain, no matter how many you add. This is just one example where your architecture can have a large effect on your ability to add capacity.

Expanding database-driven web applications might take different paths in their evolution toward scalable maturity. Some may choose to federate data across many master databases. They may split up the database into their own clusters, or choose to cache data in a variety of methods to reduce load on their database layer. Yet others may take a hybrid approach, using all of these methods of scaling. This book is not intended to be an advice column on database scaling, it's meant to serve as a guide by which you can come up with your own planning and measurement process—one that is right for your environment.

Make Your System Stats Tell Stories

Server statistics paint only part of the picture of your system's health. Unless they can be tied to actual site metrics, server statistics don't mean very much in terms of characterizing your usage. And this is something you'll need to know in order to track how capacity will change over time.

For example, knowing your web servers are processing X requests per second is handy, but it's also good to know what those X requests per second actually mean in terms of your users. Maybe X requests per second represents Y number of users employing the site simultaneously.

It would be even better to know that of those Y simultaneous users, A percent are uploading photos, B percent are making comments on a heated forum topic, and C percent are poking randomly around the site while waiting for the pizza guy to arrive. Measuring those user metrics over time is a first step. Comparing and graphing the web server hits-per-second against those user interaction metrics will ultimately yield some of the cost of providing service to the users. In the examples above, the ability to generate a comment within the application might consume more resources than simply browsing the site, but it consumes less when compared to uploading a photo. Having some idea of which features tax your capacity more than others gives you context in which to decide where you'll want to focus priority attention in your capacity planning process. These observations can also help drive any technology procurement justifications.

Quite often, the person approving expensive hardware and software requests is not the same person making the requests. Finance and business leaders must sometimes trust implicitly that their engineers are providing accurate information when they request capital for resources. Tying system statistics to business metrics helps bring the technology closer to the business units, and can help engineers understand what the growth means in terms of business success. Marrying these two metrics together can therefore help the awareness that technology costs shouldn't automatically be considered a cost center, but rather a significant driver of revenue. It also means that future capital expenditure costs have some real context, so even those non-technical folks will understand the value technology investment brings.

For example, when presenting a proposal for an order of new database hardware, you should have the systems and application metrics on hand to justify the investment. But if you had the pertinent supporting data, you could say something along the lines of "…and if we get these new database servers, we'll be able to serve our pages X percent faster, which means our pageviews—and corresponding ad revenues—have an opportunity to increase up to Y percent." Backing up your justifications in this way can also help the business development people understand what success means in terms of capacity management.

MEASURE, MEASURE, MEASURE

Engineers like graphs for good reason: they tell a story better than numbers can by themselves, and let you know exactly how your system is performing. There are some industry-tested tools and techniques used in measuring system statistics, such as CPU, memory, and disk usage. A lot of them can be reused to measure anything you need, including application-level or business metrics.

Another theme in this book is measurement, which should be considered a necessity, not an option. You have a fuel gauge on your car's dashboard for a reason. Don't make the mistake of not installing one on your systems.

We'll see more about this in Chapter 3.

Buying Stuff: Procurement Is a Process

After you've completed all your measurements, made snap judgments about usage, and sketched out future predictions, you'll need to actually buy things: bandwidth, storage appliances, servers, maybe even *instances* of virtual servers. In each case, you'll need to explain to the people with the checkbooks why you need what you think you need, and why you need it when you think you need it. (We'll talk more about predicting the future and presenting those findings in Chapter 4.)

Procurement is a process, and should be treated as yet another part of capacity planning. Whether it's a call to a hosting provider to bring new capacity online, a request for quotes from a vendor, or a trip to your local computer store, you need to take this important segment of time into account.

Smaller companies, while usually a lot less "liquid" than their larger bretheren, can really shine in this arena. Being small often goes hand-in-hand with being nimble. So while you might not be offered the best price on equipment as the big companies who buy in massive bulk, you'll likely be able to get it faster, owing to a less cumbersome approval process.

Quite often the person you might need to persuade is the CFO, who sits across the hall from you. In the early days of Flickr, we used to be able to get quotes from a vendor and simply walk over to the founder of the company (seated 20 feet away), who could cut and send a check. The servers would arrive in about a week, and we'd rack them in the data center the day they came out of the box. Easy!

Yahoo! has a more involved cycle of vetting hardware requests that includes obtaining many levels of approval and coordinating delivery to various data centers around the world. Purchases having been made, the local site operation teams in each data center then must assemble, rack, cable, and install operating systems on each of the boxes. This all takes more time than when we were a startup. Of course, the flip side is, with such a large company we can leverage buying power. By buying in bulk, we can afford a larger amount of hardware for a better price.

In either case, the concern is the same: the procurement process should be baked into your larger planning exercise. It takes time and effort, just like all the other steps. There is more about this in Chapter 4.

Performance and Capacity: Two Different Animals

The relationship between performance tuning and capacity planning is often misunderstood. While they affect each other, they have different goals. Performance tuning optimizes your *existing* system for better performance. Capacity planning determines what your system needs and when it needs it, using your current performance as a baseline.

Let's face it: tuning is fun, and it's addictive. But after you spend some time tweaking values, testing, and tweaking some more, it can become a endless hole, sucking away time and energy for little or no gain. There are those rare and beautiful times when you stumble upon some obvious and simple parameter that can make everything faster—you find the one MySQL configuration parameter that doubles the cache size, or realize after some testing that those TCP window sizes set in the kernel can really make a difference. Great! But as illustrated in Figure 1-3, for each of those rare gems you discover, the amount of obvious optimizations you find thereafter dwindles pretty rapidly.

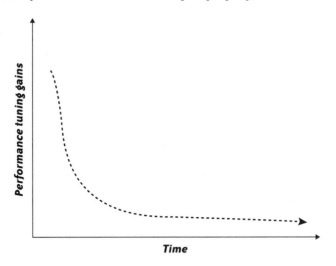

FIGURE 1-3. Decreasing returns from performance tuning

Capacity planning must happen *without* regard to what you might optimize. The first real step in the process is to accept the system's *current* performance, in order to estimate what you'll need in the future. If at some point down the road you discover some tweak that brings about more resources, that's a bonus.

Here's a quick example of the difference between performance and capacity. Suppose there is a butcher in San Francisco who prepares the most delectable bacon in the state of California. Let's assume the butcher shop has an arrangement with a store in San Jose to sell their great bacon there. Every day, the butcher needs to transport the bacon from San Francisco to San Jose using some number of trucks—and the bacon has to get there within an hour. The butcher needs to determine what type of trucks, and how many of them he'll need to get the bacon to San Jose. The demand for the bacon in San Jose is increasing with time. It's hard having the best bacon in the state, but it's a good problem to have.

The butcher has three trucks that suffice for the moment. But he knows he might be doubling the amount of bacon he'll need to transport over the next couple of months. At this point, he can either:

- Make the trucks go faster

- Get more trucks

You're probably seeing the point here. While the butcher might squeeze some extra horsepower out of the trucks by having them tuned up—or by convincing the drivers to break the speed limit—he's not going to achieve the same efficiency gain that would come from simply purchasing more trucks. He has no choice but to accept the performance of each truck, and work from there.

The moral of this little story? When faced with the question of capacity, try to ignore those urges to make existing gear faster, and focus instead on the topic at hand: finding out what you need, and when.

One other note about performance tuning and capacity: there is no silver bullet formula to tell you when tuning is appropriate and when it's not. It may be that simply buying more hardware is the correct thing to do, when weighed against engineering time spent on tuning the existing system. Striking this balance between optimization and capacity deployment is a challenge and will differ from environment to environment.

The Effects of Social Websites and Open APIs

As more and more websites install Web 2.0 characteristics, web operations are becoming increasingly important, especially capacity management. If your site contains content generated by your users, utilization and growth isn't completely under the control of the site's creators—a large portion of that control is in the hands of the user community, as shown by my example in the Preface concerning the London subway bombing. This can be scary for people accustomed to building sites with very predictable growth patterns, because it means capacity is hard to predict and needs to be on the radar of all those invested—both the business and the technology staff. The challenge for development and operations staff of a social website is to stay ahead of the growing usage by collecting enough data from that upward spiral to drive informed planning for the future.

ARCHITECTURE AND ITS EFFECT ON CAPACITY

Your driving style affects your car's mileage. A similar principle can be applied to web architectures. One of the recurring themes in this book will be how your website's architecture can have a significant impact on how you use, consume, and manage capacity. Design has greater effect on the effective use of your capacity than any tuning and tweaking of your servers and network. Design also plays a large role in how easily and flexibly you can add or subtract capacity as the need arises.

Although software and hardware tuning, optimization, and performance tweaking are related to capacity planning, they are not the same thing. This book focuses on tuning your architecture to allow for easier capacity management. Keeping the pieces of your architecture easily divisible and segmented can help you tackle a lot of load characterization problems—problems you'll need to solve before you can create an accurate picture of what will be required to grow, and when.

Providing web services via open APIs introduces a another ball of wax altogether, as your application's data will be accessed by yet more applications, each with their own usage and growth patterns. It also means users have a convenient way to abuse the system, which puts more uncertainty into the capacity equation. API usage needs to be monitored to watch for emerging patterns, usage edge cases, and rogue application developers bent on crawling the entire database tree. Controls need to be in place to enforce the guidelines or *Terms of Service* (TOS), which should accompany any open API web service (more about that in Chapter 3).

In my first year of working at Flickr, we grew from 60 photo uploads per minute to 660. We expanded from consuming 200 gigabytes of disk space per day to 880, and we ballooned from serving 3,000 images a second to 8,000. And that was just in the first year.

Capacity planning can become very important, very quickly. But it's not all that hard; all you need to do is pay a little attention to the right factors. The rest of the chapters in this book will show you how to do this. I'll split up this process into segments:

1. Determining your goals (Chapter 2)

2. Collecting metrics and finding your limits (Chapter 3)

3. Plotting out the trends and making forecasts based on those metrics and limits (Chapter 4)

4. Deploying and managing the capacity (Chapter 5)

CHAPTER TWO

Setting Goals for Capacity

YOU WOULDN'T BEGIN MIXING CONCRETE BEFORE YOU KNEW WHAT YOU WERE BUILDING. SIMILARLY, you shouldn't begin planning for capacity before you determine your site's requirements. Capacity planning involves a lot of assumptions related to why you need the capacity. Some of those assumptions are obvious, others are not.

For example, if you don't know that you *should* be serving your pages in less than three seconds, you're going to have a tough time determining how many servers you'll need to satisfy that requirement. More important, it will be even tougher to determine how many servers you'll need to add as your traffic grows.

Common sense, right? Yes, but it's amazing how many organizations don't take the time to assemble a rudimentary list of operational requirements. Waiting until users complain about slow responses or time-outs isn't a good strategy.

Establishing the acceptable speed or reliability of each part of your site can be a considerable undertaking, but it will pay off when you're planning for growth and need to know what standard you should maintain. This chapter shows you how to understand the different types of requirements your management and customers will force you to deal with, and how architectural design helps you with this planning.

Different Kinds of Requirements and Measurements

Now that we're talking about requirements—which might be set by others, external to your group—we can look at the different types you'll need to deal with. Your managers, your end-users, and your clients running websites with you, all have varying objectives and measure success in different ways. Ultimately, these requirements, or capacity goals, are interrelated and can be distilled into the following:

- Performance
  - External service monitoring
  - Business requirements
  - User expectations
- Capacity
  - System metrics
  - Resource ceilings

Interpreting Formal Measurements

Your site should be available not only to your colleagues performing tests on your website from a facility down the road, but also to real visitors who may be located on other continents with slow connections. Some large companies choose to have site performance (and availability) constantly monitored by services such as Keynote (*http://keynote.com*) or Gomez (*http://gomez.com*). These commercial services deploy worldwide networks of machines that constantly ping your web pages to record the return time. Servers then keep track of all these metrics and build you a handy-dandy dashboard to evaluate how your site performance and uptime appears from many locations around the world. Because Keynote and Gomez are deemed "objective" third parties, those statistics can be used to enforce or guide Service Level Agreements (SLAs) arranged with partner companies or sites (we'll talk more about SLAs later). Keynote and Gomez can be considered enterprise-level services. There are also plenty of low-cost alternatives, including PingDom (*http://pingdom.com*), SiteUptime (*http://siteuptime.com*), and Alertra (*http://alertra.com*).

It's important to understand exactly what these services measure, and how to interpret the numbers they generate. Since most of them are networks of *machines* rather than people, it's essential to be aware of how those web pages are being requested. Some things to consider when you're looking at service monitoring systems include:

- Are they simulating human users?
- Are they caching objects like a normal web browser would? Why or why not?
- Can you determine how much time is spent due to network transfer versus server time, both in the aggregate, and for each object?
- Can you determine whether a failure or unexpected wait time is due to geographic network issues or measurement failures?

If you believe your service monitoring systems are testing in a manner representative of your users when they visit your site, you have good reasons to trust the numbers. Also keep in mind, the metrics you use for capacity planning or site performance measurement might ultimately find their way onto an executive dashboard somewhere, viewed by a non-technical audience.

CFOs, CTOs, business development folks, and even CEOs can become addicted to qualitative assessments of operations. This can be a double-edged sword. On the one hand, you're being transparent about failures, which can help when you're attempting to justify expenditures and organizational changes to support capacity. On the other hand, you're also giving a frequently obsessive crowd more to obsess about, so when there are any anomalies in this data, you should be prepared to explain what they mean.

Service Level Agreements

So what exactly is an SLA? It's an instrument that makes business people comfortable, much like insurance. But in broader, less anxious terms, an SLA is a metric that defines how a service should operate within agreed-upon boundaries. It puts some financial muscle into the metric by establishing a schedule of credits for meeting goals, or possibly penalties if the service does not achieve them. With websites, SLAs cover mostly *availability* and *performance*.

Some SLAs guarantee a service will available for a pre-established percentage of time, such as 99.99%. What this means is that 0.01% of the time, the service can be unavailable, and it will still be within the bounds of the SLA. Other SLAs require that demand for a service stay within reasonable limits; request rate limits or storage and upload limits are typical parameters.

For example, you might find a web hosting company with something like verbiage below in its "Terms of Service" document:

Acme Hosting, Inc. will use commercially reasonable efforts to make the SuperHostingPlan available with a Monthly uptime percentage (defined below) of at least 99.9% during any monthly billing cycle. In the event Acme Hosting, Inc. does not meet this commitment, you will be eligible to receive a service credit as described below.

Monthly uptime percentage	Credit percentage
Between 99 and 99.9%	1 day credit
Less than 99%	1 week credit

Looks pretty reassuring, doesn't it? The problem is, 99.9% uptime stretched over a month isn't as great a number as one might think:

30 days = 720 hours = 43,200 minutes
99.9% of 43,200 minutes = 43,156.8 minutes
43,200 minutes – 43,156.8 minutes = 43.2 minutes

This means for 43.2 minutes every month, this service can go down without penalty. If your site generates $3,000 worth of sales every minute, you could easily calculate how much money any amount of downtime will cost you (along with the less measurable consequence of disgruntled customers). Table 2-1 shows percentages of uptime on a yearly basis.

TABLE 2-1. SLA percentages and acceptable downtimes

Uptime SLA	Downtime per year
90.0%	36 days, 12 hours
95.0%	18 days, 6 hours
99.0%	87 hours, 36 minutes
99.50%	43 hours, 48 minutes
99.90%	8 hours, 45 minutes, 36 seconds
99.99%	52 minutes, 33 seconds
99.999%	5 minutes, 15 seconds
99.9999%	32 seconds

The term *five-nines* is commonly heard in discussions about SLAs and availability. This refers to 99.999% availability, and it is used in marketing literature at least as much as it is in technical literature. Five-nines is usually used to indicate your site or system is deemed to be *highly* available.

These SLA availability numbers aim to provide a level of confidence in a website's service, but also imply you can equate downtime to lost revenue. I don't believe this is actually accurate, as the straight math will bear out. If your service is unavailable for 10 minutes and it normally produces $3,000 of revenue every minute, then you might assume your business has lost $30,000. In reality, customers might just pick up where they left off and buy what they were in the process of buying when the outage occurred. Your business might be spending extra money on the customer service side to make up for an outage that has no impact on your earnings.

The point is, while a true and accurate financial representation of an outage may be neither true nor accurate, the importance of availability should be clear.

Business Capacity Requirements

The use of *web services* is becoming more and more prevalent in today's Web 2.0 mashup-y world. While most web services offer open APIs for individual application developers to build upon, business-to-business relationships depend on them as well. Therefore, companies usually tie revenue streams to having unfettered access to an API. This could mean a business relationship relies on a certain level of availability, or performance of your API, measured in a percentage uptime (such as 99.99%) or an agreed-upon rate of API requests.

Let's assume your website provides postal codes, given various inputs to the API you've built. You might allow only one API call per minute to a regular or non-commercial user, but a shipping company might enter into a contract permitting it to call your API up to 10 times per *second*. Website capacity planning is as much about justifying capital expenditures as it is about technical issues, such as scaling, architectures, software, and hardware. Because capacity concerns can have such a large impact on *business* operations, they should be considered early in the process of development.

User Expectations

Obviously, the end goal of capacity planning is a smooth and speedy experience for your users. Several factors can affect the user's experience beside capacity. It's possible to have plenty of capacity but a slow website nonetheless. Designing fast web pages is beyond the scope of this book, but you can find a lot of great information in Steve Souders' excellent book, *High Performance Web Sites* (O'Reilly).

Even though capacity is only one part of making the end-user experience fast, that experience is still one of the real-world metrics that we'll want to measure and track in order to make forecasts.

For example, when serving static web content, you may reach an intolerable amount of latency at high volumes before any system-level metrics (CPU, disk, memory) raise a red flag. Again, this can have more to do with the construction of the web page than the capacity of the servers sending the content. But as capacity is one of the more expensive pieces to change, it warrants investigation. Perceived slowness of a web page *could* be the result of a page that is simply too heavy, and not from a lack of capacity. (This is one of the fundamentals of Souders' book.) It's a good idea to determine whether this is the case when any user-perceived slowness is analyzed. The problem can be solved by either 1) adding capacity, or, 2) changing the page weight. The first solution can sometimes involve more cost than solution two.

At Flickr, we serve tens of thousands of photos per second. Each photo server can serve a known and specific rate of images before reaching its maximum. We don't define this maximum in terms of disk I/O, or CPU, or memory, but in terms of how many images we can serve without the "time to serve" for each image exceeding the specified amount of time.

Architecture Decisions

Your architecture is the basic layout of how all of the backend pieces—both hardware and software—are joined. Its design plays a crucial role in your ability to plan and manage capacity. Designing the architecture can be a complex undertaking, but there are a couple of great books available to help you: Cal Henderson's *Building Scalable Web Sites* (O'Reilly) and Theo Schlossnagle's *Scalable Internet Architectures* (Pearson).

Your architecture affects nearly every part of performance, reliability, and management. Establishing good architecture almost always translates to easier effort when planning for capacity.

Providing Measurement Points

Both for measurements purposes as well as for rapid response to changing conditions, you want your architecture to be designed so you can easily split it into parts that perform discrete tasks. In an ideal world, each component of the backend should have a single job to do, but it could still do multiple jobs well, if needed. At the same time, its effectiveness on each job should be easy to measure.

For instance, let's look at a simple, database-driven web application just starting on its path toward world domination. To get the most bang for our buck, we have our web server and our database residing on the same hardware server. This means all the moving parts share the same hardware resources, as shown in Figure 2-1.

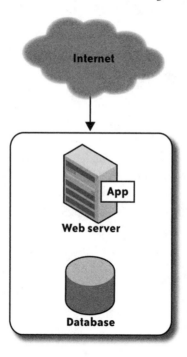

FIGURE 2-1. A simple, single-server web application architecture

Let's suppose you've already read Chapter 3 (cheating, are we?) and you have configured measurements for both system and application-level statistics for your server. You can measure the system statistics of this server via sar or rrdtool, and maybe even application-level measurements such as web resource requests or database queries-per-second.

The difficulty with the setup in Figure 2-1 is you can't easily distinguish which system statistics correspond with the different pieces of the architecture. Therefore, you can't answer basic questions that are likely to arise, such as:

- Is the disk utilization the result of the web server sending out a lot of static content from the disk, or rather, the database's queries being disk-bound?

- How much of the filesystem cache, CPU, memory, and disk utilization is being consumed by the web server, and how much is being used for the database?

With careful research, you can make some estimates about which daemon is using which resource. In the best case, the resource demands of the different daemons don't contend with one another. For example, the web server might be bound mostly by CPU and not need much memory, whereas the database might be memory-bound without using much CPU. But even in this ideal scenario, if usage continues to grow, the resource contention will grow to warrant splitting the architecture into different hardware components (Figure 2-2). At that point, you'd really like to know how much CPU, cache, disk space, bus bandwidth, and so on, each daemon actually needs.

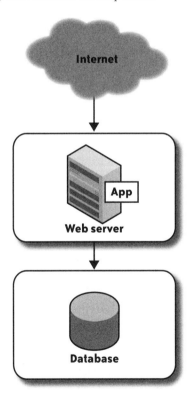

FIGURE 2-2. Separation of web server and database

Splitting the nodes in this fashion makes it easier to understand the capacity demands, as the resources on each server are now dedicated to each piece of the architecture. It also means you can measure each server and its resource demands more distinctly. You could come to conclusions with the single-component configuration, but with less ease and accuracy. Of course, this division of labor also produces performance gains, such as preventing frontend client-side traffic from interfering with database traffic, but let's forget about performance for the moment.

If we're recording system and application-level statistics, you can quantify what each unit of capacity means in terms of usage. With this new architecture, you can answer a few questions that you couldn't before, such as:

Database server
How do increases in database queries-per-second affect the following?

- Disk utilization
- I/O Wait (percent of time the database waits due to network or disk operations)
- RAM usage
- CPU usage

Web server
How do increases in web server requests-per-second affect the following?

- Disk utilization
- I/O Wait
- RAM usage
- CPU usage

Being able to answer these questions is key to establishing how (and when) you'll want to add more capacity to each piece.

Providing Scaling Points

Now that you have a good idea of what's required for each piece of this simple architecture, you can get a sense for whether you'll want different hardware configurations.

At Flickr, for the most part, our MySQL database installations happen to be disk-bound, so there's no compelling reason to buy two quad-core CPUs for each database box. Instead, we spend money on more disk spindles and memory to help with filesystem performance and caching. We know this to be our ideal database hardware configuration—for our database. We have different configurations for our image serving machines, our web servers, and our image processing machines; all according to what in-box resources they rely on most.

The last piece we're missing in this discussion on architecture is what drives capacity forecasting: *resource ceilings*. The questions posed earlier regarding the effects of usage on resources, point to an obvious culmination: *when will the database or web server die?*

Each server in our example possesses a finite amount of the following hardware resources:

- Disk throughput
- Disk storage
- CPU
- RAM
- Network

High loads will bump against the limits of one or more of those resources. Somewhere just below that critical level is where you'll want to determine your *ceiling* for each piece of your architecture. Your ceiling is the critical level of a particular resource (or resources) that cannot be crossed without failure. Armed with your current ceilings, you can start to assemble your capacity plan. We'll talk more about examples of ceilings in Chapter 3.

As you can see, changing architecture in simple ways can help you understand for what purposes your capacity is being used. When thinking about architecture design, keep in mind the division of labor and the "small pieces, loosely joined" theory can go a long way toward giving you clues as to how your site is being used. We'll touch more on architecture decisions throughout the book, and particularly in Chapter 3.

Hardware Decisions (Vertical, Horizontal, and Diagonal Scaling)

Choosing the right hardware for each component of your architecture can greatly affect costs. At the very least, when it comes to servers, you should have a basic idea (gleaned from measurement and usage patterns) of where you want to invest your money.

Before perusing your vendor's current pricing, be aware of what you're trying to achieve. Will this server be required to do a lot of CPU work? Will it need to perform a lot of memory work? Is it a network-bound gateway?

Today, the difference between horizontal and vertical scaling architectures are quite well known in the industry, but it bears reviewing in order to put capacity planning into context.

Being able to scale *horizontally* means having an architecture that allows for adding capacity by simply adding similarly functioning nodes to the existing infrastructure. For instance, a second web server to share the burden of website visits.

Being able to scale *vertically* is the capability of adding capacity by increasing the resources internal to a server, such as CPU, memory, disk, and network.

Since the emergence of tiered and *shared-nothing* architectures, horizontal scaling has been widely recognized for its advantages over vertical scaling as it pertains to web applications. Being able to scale horizontally means designing your application to handle various levels of database abstraction and distribution. You can find great approaches to horizontal application development techniques in the aforementioned books by Henderson and Schlossnagle.

The danger of relying *solely* on vertical scaling is, as you continue to upgrade components of a single computer, the cost rises dramatically. You also introduce the risk of a *single point of failure* (SPOF).

Horizontal scaling involves the more complex issue of increasing the potential failure points as you expand the size of the server farm. In addition, you inherently introduce some challenges surrounding any synchronization you'll need between the nodes.

Diagonal scaling (a term coined by myself) is the process of vertically scaling the horizontally scaled nodes you already have in your infrastructure. Over time, CPU power and RAM become faster, cheaper, and cooler, and disk storage becomes larger and less expensive, so it can be cost effective to keep some vertical scaling as part of your plan, but applied to horizontal nodes.

What this all boils down to is, for all of your nodes bound on CPU or RAM, you can "upgrade" to fewer servers with more CPU and RAM. For disk-bound boxes, it can also mean you may be able to replace them with fewer machines that have more disk spindles.

As an example, I'll take a recent Flickr upgrade.

Initially, we had 67 dual-CPU, 4 GB RAM, single SATA drive web servers. For the most part, our frontend layer is CPU-bound, handling requests from client browsers, making backend database calls, and taking photo uploads. These 67 machines were equipped with Intel Xeon 2.80 GHz CPUs running Apache and PHP.

When it was time to add capacity, we decided to try the new Quad Core CPU boxes. We found the dual quad core machines had roughly three times the processing power of the existing dual CPU boxes. With 8 CPU cores of Intel Xeon L5320 1.86 GHz CPUs, we were able to replace 67 existing boxes with only 18 new boxes. Figure 2-3 illustrates how much the server load average (across the entire cluster) dropped as a result.

Figure 2-3 shows the reduction in load average when the 67 machines were removed from the production pool and the 18 new boxes were allowed to take over for the same production load. This certainly makes for a very dramatic-looking graph, but load average might not be the best metric to illustrate this diagonal scaling exercise.

Figure 2-4 represents the same time period as Figure 2-3, except it details the number of apache requests-per-second when the older servers were replaced. The shades of lines on the graph represent a single server, allowing you to clearly see when the newer servers took over. Note the amount of apache requests-per-second actually went up by as much as 400 after the replacement, implying the older machines were very close to their own bottlenecks.

Let's take a look at Table 2-2 to learn what this meant in terms of resources.

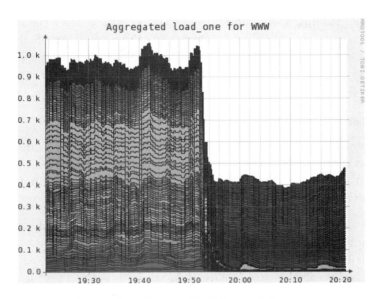

FIGURE 2-3. Load average drop by replacing 67 boxes with 18 higher capacity boxes

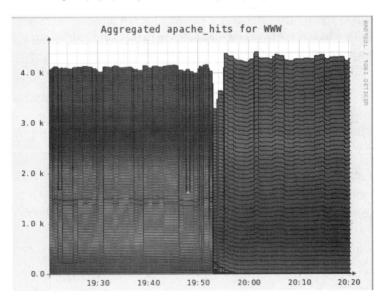

FIGURE 2-4. Serving more traffic with fewer servers

TABLE 2-2. Comparing server architectures

Servers	CPU	RAM	Disk	Power (kW) at 60% of peak usage
67	2 (2 cores)	4 GB	1 x 80 GB SATA	8.763
18	2 (8 cores)	4 GB	1 x 146 GB SATA	2.332

Based on traffic patterns, if we assume the servers are working at an average of about 60 percent of their peak, this means we're using roughly 30 percent of the electrical power we were using previously. We've also saved 49U of rack space because each server needs only 1U of space. That's more than one full, standard 42U rack emptied as a result of diagonal scaling. Not bad.

Disaster Recovery

Disaster recovery is saving business operations (along with other resources, such as data, which we won't consider in this book) after a natural or human-induced catastrophe. By catastrophe, I'm not implying the failure of a single server, but a complete outage that's usually external to the operation of the website infrastructure.

Examples of such disasters include data center power or cooling outages, as well as physical disasters, such as earthquakes. It can also include incidents, such as construction accidents or explosions that affect the power, cooling, or network connectivity relied upon by your site. Regardless of the cause, the effect is the same: you can't serve your website. Continuing to serve traffic under failure conditions is obviously an important part of web operations and architecture design. Contingency planning clearly involves capacity management. *Disaster recovery* (DR) is only one part of what is termed *Business Continuity Planning* (BCP), which is the larger logistical plan to ensure continuity of business in the face of different failure event scenarios.

In most cases, the solution is to deploy complete architectures in two (or more) separate physical locations, which means multiplying your infrastructure costs. It also means multiplying the nodes you'll need to manage, doubling all of the data replication, code, and configuration deployment, and multiplying all of your monitoring and measurement applications by the number of data centers you deploy.

Clearly, DR plans raise both economic and technical concerns. DR and BCP are large topics in and of themselves, and are beyond the scope of this book. If this topic is of particular interest to you, there are many books available dedicated specifically to this subject.

CHAPTER THREE

Measurement: Units of Capacity

**The only man who behaves sensibly is my tailor; he takes my
measurements anew every time he sees me, while all the rest
go on with their old measurements and expect me to fit them.**

—*George Bernard Shaw*

IF YOU DON'T HAVE A WAY TO MEASURE YOUR CURRENT CAPACITY, YOU CAN'T CONDUCT CAPACITY
planning—you'll only be guessing. Fortunately, a seemingly endless range of tools is available for measuring computer performance and usage. I'm willing to bet that moments
after the first computer program was written, another one was written to measure and
record how fast the first one performed.

Most operating systems come with some basic built-in utilities that can measure various
performance and consumption metrics. Most of these utilities usually provide a way to
record results as well. Additional popular open source tools are easy to download and run
on virtually any modern system. For capacity planning, your measurement tools should
provide, at minimum, an easy way to:

- Record and store data over time
- Build custom metrics
- Compare metrics from various sources
- Import and export metrics

As long as you choose tools that can in some way satisfy this criteria, you don't need to spend much time pondering which to use. What is more important is what metrics you choose to measure, and what metrics to which you pay particular attention.

In this chapter, I'll discuss the specific statistics you'll want to measure for different purposes, and show the results in graphs to help you better interpret them. There are plenty of other sources of information on how to set up particular tools to generate the measurements; most professional system administrators already have such tools installed.

ACCEPTING THE OBSERVER EFFECT

Measuring your systems introduces yet another task your server will be asked to perform in order to function properly. Some system resources are going to be consumed for the purposes of collection and transfer of metrics. Good monitoring tools make an effort to be lightweight and not get in the way of a server's primary work, but there will always be some amount of overhead. This means simply measuring your system's resources will in some small way (hopefully, very small) affect the system's behavior, and by extension, the very measurements you end up recording. This is commonly known as the "observer effect."

My philosophy is to accept the burden on the server and the slight distortion in the data collected as a cost of doing business. Giving up some percentage of CPU, disk, memory, and network resources to provide clear and useful measurement data is a small price to pay for monitoring your system's overall health and capacity.

Aspects of Capacity Tracking Tools

This chapter is about automatically and routinely measuring server behavior over a predefined amount of time. By monitoring normal behavior over days, weeks, and months, you'll be able to see both patterns that recur regularly, and trends over time that help you predict when you need to increase capacity.

We'll also discuss deliberately increasing the load through artificial scaling using methods that closely simulate what will happen to your site in the future. This will also help you predict the need to increase capacity.

For the tasks in this chapter, you need tools that collect, store, and display (usually on a graph) metrics over time. They can be used to drive capacity predictions as well as problem resolution.

Examples of these tools include:

Cacti (*http://cacti.net*)
Munin (*http://munin.projects.linpro.no/*)
Ganglia (*http://ganglia.info*)
Hyperic HQ (*http://hyperic.com*)

The tools don't need to be fancy. In fact, for some metrics, I still simply load them into Excel and plot them there. Appendix C contains a more comprehensive list of capacity planning tools.

It's important to start out by understanding the types of monitoring to which this chapter refers. Companies in the web operations field use the term *monitoring* to describe all sorts of operations—generating alerts concerning system availability, data collection and its analysis, real-world and artificial end user interaction measurement—the list goes on and on. Quite often this causes confusion. I suspect many commercial vendors who align on any one of those areas exploit this confusion to further their own goals, much to our detriment as end users.

This chapter is *not* concerned with system availability, the health of your servers, or notification management—the sorts of activities offered by Nagios, Zenoss, OpenNMS, and other popular network monitoring systems. Some of these tools do offer some of the features we need for our monitoring purposes, such as the ability to display and store metrics. But they exist mostly to help you recognize urgent problems and avoid imminent disasters. For the most part, they function a lot like extremely complex alarm clocks and smoke detectors.

Metric collection systems, on the other hand, act more like court reporters, who observe and record what's going on without taking any action whatsoever. As it pertains to our goals, the term monitoring refers to metric collection systems used to collect, store, and display system and application-level metrics of your infrastructure.

Fundamentals and Elements of Metric Collection Systems

Nearly every major commercial and open source metric collection system employs the same architecture. As depicted in Figure 3-1, this architecture usually consists of an *agent* that runs on each of the physical machines being monitored, and a single *server* that aggregates and displays the metrics. As the number of nodes in your infrastructure grows, you will probably have more than a single server performing aggregation, especially in the case of multiple data center operations.

The agent's job is to periodically collect data from the machine on which it's running and send a summary to the metric aggregation server. The metric aggregation server stores the metrics for each of the machines it's monitoring, which can then be displayed by various methods. Most aggregation servers use some sort of database; one specialized format known as *Round-Robin Database* (RRD) is particularly popular.

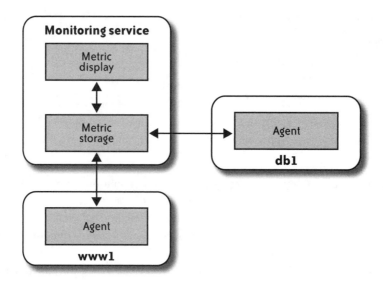

FIGURE 3-1. The fundamental pieces of most metric collection systems

Round-Robin Database and RRDTool

RRDTool is probably the most commonly used utility for storing system and network data—at least for those using the LAMP stack. I'm only going to offer you an overview here, but you can find a full description of it on the "about" page and in the tutorials of its RRDTool website at *http://rrdtool.org*.

The key characteristics of system monitoring data concern its size: there's a lot of it, and it's constantly increasing. Thus, ironically, you need to do capacity planning just for the data you're collecting for capacity planning! The Round-Robin Database (RRDTool) utility solves that by making an assumption that you're interested in fine details only for the recent past. As you move backward in the stored data, it's acceptable to lose some of the details. After some maximum time defined by the user (say, a year), you let data disappear completely. This approach sets a finite limit on how much data you're storing, with the tradeoff being the degree of detail as time moves on.

RRDTool can also be used to generate graphs from this data and show views on the various time slices for which you've recorded data. It also contains utilities to dump, restore, and manipulate RRD data, which come in handy when you drill down into some of the nitty-gritty details of capacity measurement. The metric collection tools mentioned earlier in "Aspects of Capacity Tracking Tools" are frontends to RRDTool.

Ganglia

The charts in this chapter were generated by Ganglia (*http://ganglia.info*). I had several reasons for choosing this frontend to present examples and illustrate useful monitoring practices. First, Ganglia is the tool we currently use for this type of monitoring at Flickr.

We chose it based partly on some general reasons that might make it a good choice for you as well: it's powerful (offering good support for the criteria I listed at the beginning of the chapter) and popular. But in addition, Ganglia was developed originally as a grid management and measurement mechanism aimed at high performance computing (HPC) clusters. Ganglia works well for Flickr's infrastructure because our architecture is similar to HPC environments, in that our backend is segmented into different clusters of machines that each play a different role.

The principles in this chapter, however, are valuable regardless of which monitoring tool you use. Fundamentally, Ganglia works similarly to most metric collection and storage tools. Its metric collection agent is called *gmond* and the aggregation server piece is called *gmetad*. The metrics are displayed using a PHP-based web interface.

SNMP

The Simple Network Management Protocol (SNMP) is a common mechanism for gathering metrics for most networking and server equipment. Think of SNMP as a standardized monitoring and metric collection protocol. Most routers, switches, and servers support it.

SNMP collects and sends more types of metrics than most administrators choose to measure. Because most networking equipment and embedded devices are closed systems, you can't run user-installed applications, such as a metric collection agent like *gmond*. However, as SNMP has long been a standard for networking devices, it provides an easy way to extract metrics from those devices without depending on an agent.

Treating Logs As Past Metrics

Logs are a great way to inject metrics into your measurement systems, and it underscores one of our criteria for being able to create custom metrics within your monitoring system.

Web servers can log a wealth of information. When you see a spike in resources on a graph, you can often drill down to the access and error logs to find the exact moment those resources jumped. Thus, logs make problem identification easier. Most databases have options to log queries that exceed a certain amount of time, allowing you to identify and fix those slow-running queries. Almost everything you use—mail servers, load balancers, firewalls–has the ability to create logs, either directly or via a Unix-style syslog facility. As an example, at Flickr we count the number of web server error and access log lines per minute and include those metrics into Ganglia's graphs.

Monitoring As a Tool for Urgent Problem Identification

As will be mentioned in the upcoming section, "Applications of Monitoring," problem notification is a separate area of expertise from capacity planning, and generally uses different tools. But some emerging problems are too subtle to trigger health checks from tools such as Nagios. However, the tools we cover in this chapter can be pressed into service to warn you of impending trouble. The techniques in this section can also quickly show you the effects of an optimization.

Figure 3-2 shows some anomalous behavior we once discovered on Flickr through Ganglia. It represents several high-level views of some of Flickr's clusters.

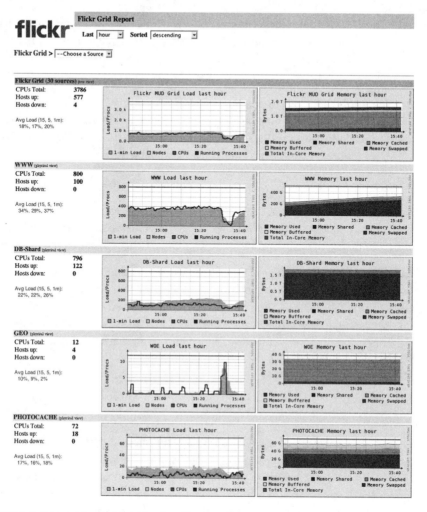

FIGURE 3-2. Using metric collection to identify problems

Without even looking into the details, you can see from the graphs on the left that something unusual has just happened. These graphs cover the load and running processes on the cluster, whereas the groups on the right display combined reports on the memory usage for those clusters. The X axes for all of the graphs correspond to the same time period, so it's quite easy to see the number of running processes (notably in the WWW cluster) dip in conjunction with the spike in the GEO cluster.

The WWW cluster obviously contains Apache frontend machines serving flickr.com, and our GEO cluster is a collection of servers that perform geographic lookups for features such as photo geotagging. By looking at this one web page, I can ascertain where the problem originated (GEO) and where its effects were felt (all other clusters). As it turns out, this particular event occurred when one of our GEO servers stalled on some of its requests. The connections from our web servers accumulated as a result. When we restarted the GEO server, the web servers gradually recovered.

When faults occur with your website, there is tremendous value in being able to quickly gather status information. You want to be able to get fast answers to the following questions:

- What was the fault?
- When did the fault occur?
- What caused the fault?

In this example, Figure 3-2 helped us pinpoint the source of the trouble because we could correlate the event's effects (via the timeline) on each of our clusters.

Network Measurement and Planning

Capacity planning goes beyond servers and storage to include the network to which they're all connected. The implementation details of routing protocols and switching architectures are not within the scope of this book, but your network is just like any of your other resource: finite in capacity, and well worth measuring.

Networks are commonly viewed as plumbing for servers, and the analogy is apt. When your network is operating well, data simply flows. When it doesn't, everything comes to a grinding halt. This isn't to say that subtle and challenging problems don't crop up with networking: far from it. But for the most part, network devices are designed to do one task well, and their limits should be clear.

Network capacity in hosted environments is often a metered and strictly controlled resource; getting data about your usage can be difficult, depending on the contract you have with your network provider. As a sanity check on your inbound and outbound network usage, aggregate your outward-facing server network metrics and compare them with the bill you receive from your hosting provider.

When you own your own racks and switches, you can make educated decisions about how to divide the hosts across them according to the network capacity they'll need. For example, at Flickr, our photo cache servers demand quite a bit from their switches, because all they do is handle requests for downloads of photos. We're careful not to put too many of them on one switch so the servers have enough bandwidth.

Routers and switches are like servers in that they have various metrics that can be extracted (usually with the SNMP protocol) and recorded. While their main metrics are the bytes *in* and *out* per second (or packets in and out if the payloads are small), they often expose other metrics as well, such as CPU usage and current network sessions.

All of these metrics should be measured on a periodic basis with a network graphing tool, such as MRTG, or some other utility that can store the history for each metric. Unlike Ganglia and other metric collection tools, MRTG is built with SNMP in mind. Simply because your switch and router are well below your limits of network capacity doesn't mean you're not nearing CPU usage ceilings on those devices—all of those metrics should be monitored with alerting thresholds as well.

Load Balancing

Load balancers have been a source of much joy and pain in the field of web operations. Their main purpose is to distribute load among pools, or clusters of machines, and they can range from the simplest to the most complex beasts in your data center. Load balancing is usually implemented on the frontend of the architecture, playing traffic cop to web servers that respond to data requests from user's browsers. But load balancers have also been used to spread load across databases, middle-layer application servers, geographically dispersed data centers, and mail servers; the list continues on.

Load balancers establish load distribution based on a relatively short list of algorithms, and enable you specify the protocols to balance across the available servers serving the traffic. *Scalable Internet Architectures* by Theo Schlossnagle (Pearson) contains some excellent insights into load balancers and their role in web architectures.

For our purposes, load balancers provide a great framework for capacity management, because they allow the easy expansion and removal of capacity in a production environment. They also offer us a place to experiment safely with various amounts of live web traffic so we can track the real effect it has on our server's resources. You'll see later why this is useful in helping to find your server's ceilings. This can be the joy found with load balancing: convenience in deploying and researching capacity.

But there is also pain. Because load balancers are such an integral part of the architecture, failures can be spectacular and dramatic. Not all situations call for load balancing. Even when load balancing is needed, not all balancing algorithms are appropriate.

Jeremy Zawodny recounted a story in the first edition of *High Performance MySQL* (O'Reilly) in which databases at Yahoo! were being load balanced with a "least connections" scheme. This scheme works quite well when balancing web servers: it ensures the server with the smallest number of requests has more traffic directed to it. The reason it works with web servers is web requests are almost always short-lived and on average don't vary to a great extent in size or latency. The paradigm falls apart, however, with databases because not all queries are the same in terms of size and time to process, and the results of those queries can be quite large. The lesson Zawodny leaves us is just because a database has relatively few current connections does not mean it can tolerate more load.

A second concern with load balancing databases is how to check the health of specific servers within the pool to determine if they all remain capable of receiving traffic. As mentioned earlier, databases are application-specific beasts, so what will work for my application might not work for yours. For me, replication slave lag may be the determining factor for health, whereas for you, it could be the current rate of SELECT statements.

Further complications in load balancing include uncommon protocols, complicated balancing algorithms, and the tuning needed to ensure load balancing is working optimally for your application.

Applications of Monitoring

The remainder of this chapter uses examples to demonstrate some of the important monitoring techniques you need to know and perform.

Application-Level Measurement

As mentioned earlier, server statistics paint only a part of the capacity picture. You should also measure and record higher-level metrics specific to your application—not specific to one server, but to the whole system. CPU and server disk usage on a web server doesn't tell the whole tale of what's happening to each web request, and a stream of web requests can involve multiple pieces of hardware.

At Flickr, we have a dashboard that collects these application-level metrics. They are collected on both a daily and cumulative basis. Some of the metrics can be drawn from a database, such as the number of photos uploaded. Others can come from aggregating some of the server statistics, such as total disk space consumed across disparate machines. Data collection techniques can be as simple as running a script from a cron job and putting results into its own database for future mining.

Some of the metrics currently tracked at Flickr are:

- Photos uploaded (daily, cumulative)
- Photos uploaded per hour
- Average photo size (daily, cumulative)
- Processing time to segregate photos based on their different sizes (hourly)
- User registrations (daily, cumulative)
- Pro account signups (daily, cumulative)
- Number of photos tagged (daily, cumulative)
- API traffic (API keys in use, requests made per second, per key)
- Number of unique tags (daily, cumulative)
- Number of geotagged photos (daily, cumulative)

We also track certain financial metrics, such as payments received (which lie outside the scope of this book). For your particular application, a good exercise would be to spend some time correlating business and financial data to the system and application metrics you're tracking.

For example, a Total Cost of Ownership (TCO) calculation would be incomplete without some indication of how much these system and application metrics cost the business.

Imagine being able to correlate the real costs to serve a single web page with your application. Having these calculations would not only put the architecture into a different context from web operations (business metrics instead of availability, or performance metrics), but they can also provide context for the more finance-obsessed, non-technical upper management who might have access to these tools.

I can't overemphasize the value inherent to identifying and tracking application metrics. Your efforts will be rewarded by imbuing your system statistics with context beyond server health, and will help guide your forecasts. During the procurement process, TCO calculations will prove to be invaluable, as we'll see later.

Now that we've covered the basics of capacity measurement, let's take a look at which measurements you—the manager of a potentially fast-growing website—will likely want to pay special attention. I'll discuss the common elements of web infrastructure and list considerations for measuring their capacity and establishing their upper limits. I'll also provide some examples taken from Flickr's own capacity planning to add greater relevance. The examples are designed to illustrate useful metrics you may wish to track as well. They are not intended to suggest Flickr's architecture or implementation will fit every application's environment.

Storage Capacity

The topic of data storage is vast. For our purposes, I'm going to focus only on the segments of storage that directly influence capacity planning for a high data volume website.

One of the most effective storage analogies is that of a glass of water. The analogy combines a finite limit (the size of the glass) with a variable (the amount of water that can be put into and taken out of the glass at any given time). This helps you to visualize the two major factors to consider when choosing where and how to store your data:

- The maximum capacity of the storage media
- The rate at which the data can be accessed

Traditionally, most web operations have been concerned with the first consideration—the size of the glass. However, most commercial storage vendors have aligned their product lines with both considerations in mind. In most cases, there are two options: large, slow, inexpensive disks (usually using ATA/SATA), and smaller, fast, expensive disks (SCSI and SAS technologies).

Even though the field of data storage has matured, there are still many emerging—and possibly disruptive—technologies of which you should be aware. The popularity of solid-state drives and the hierarchical storage schemes that incorporate them may soon become the norm, as the costs of storage continue to drop and the raw I/O speed of storage has remained flat in recent years.

Consumption rates

When planning the storage needs for your application, the first and foremost consideration should be the *consumption rate*. This is the growth in your data volume measured against a specific length of time. For sites that consume, process, and store rich media files, such as images, video, and audio, keeping an eye on storage consumption rates can be critical to the business. But consumption is important to watch even if your storage doesn't grow much at all.

Disk space is about the easiest capacity metric to understand. Even the least technically inclined computer user understands what it means to run out of disk space.

For storage consumption, the central question is:

> When will I run out of disk space?

A real-world example: Tracking storage consumption

At Flickr, we consume a lot of disk space as photos are uploaded and stored. I'll use this simple case as an example of planning for storage consumption.

When photos are uploaded, they are divided into different groups based on size, and sent to a storage appliance. We collect a wide range of metrics related to this process, including:

- How much time it takes to process each image into its various sizes
- How many photos were uploaded
- The average size of the photos
- How much disk space is consumed by those photos

Later, we'll see why we chose to measure these, but for the moment our focus is on the last item: the total disk space consumption over time.

We collect and store this number on a daily basis. The daily time slice has enough detail to show weekly, monthly, seasonal, and holiday trends. Thus, it can be used to predict when we'll need to order more storage hardware. Table 3-1 presents disk space consumption (for photos only) for a two-week period in 2005.

TABLE 3-1. Sample statistics on daily disk space consumption

Date	Total usage (GB)	Daily usage (GB)
07/26/05	14321.83	138.00
07/27/05	14452.60	130.77
07/28/05	14586.54	133.93
07/29/05	14700.89	114.35
07/30/05	14845.72	144.82
07/31/05	15063.99	218.27
08/01/05	15250.21	186.21

Date	Total usage (GB)	Daily usage (GB)
08/02/05	15403.82	153.61
08/03/05	15558.81	154.99
08/04/05	15702.35	143.53
08/05/05	15835.76	133.41
08/06/05	15986.55	150.79
08/07/05	16189.27	202.72
08/08/05	16367.88	178.60

The data in Table 3-1 is derived from a cron job that runs a script to record the output from the standard Unix df command on our storage appliances. The data is then aggregated and included on a metrics dashboard. (We also collect data in much smaller increments [minutes] using Ganglia, but this is not relevant to the current example.)

When we plot the data from Table 3-1, two observations become clear, as shown in Figure 3-3.

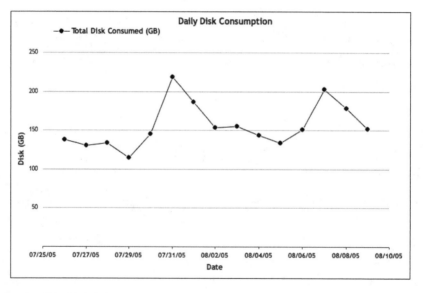

FIGURE 3-3. Table of daily disk consumption

We can quickly see that the dates 7/31 and 8/07 were high upload periods. In fact, the 31st of July and the 7th of August in 2005 were both Sundays. Indeed, metrics gathered over a long period reveal Sundays have always been the weekly peak for uploads. Another general trend that can be seen in the chart is Fridays are the lowest upload days of the week. We'll discuss trends in the next chapter, but for now, it's enough to know you should be collecting your data with an appropriate resolution to illuminate trends. Some sites show variations on an hourly basis (such as visits to news or weather information); others use monthly slices (retail sites with high-volume periods prior to Christmas).

Storage I/O patterns

How you're going to access your storage is the next most important consideration. Are you a video site requiring a considerable amount of sequential disk access? Are you using storage for a database that needs to search for fragmented bits of data stored on drives in a random fashion?

Disk utilization metrics can vary, depending on what sort of storage architecture you're trying to measure, but the basics are:

- How much you're reading
- How much you're writing
- How long your CPU is waiting for either reading or writing to finish

Disk drives are the slowest devices in a server. Depending on your server's load characteristic, these metrics could be what defines your capacity for an entire server platform. Disk utilization and throughput can be measured a number of ways. You'll find a lot of useful disk measurement tools in Appendix C.

Whether you're using RAID on a local disk subsystem, a Network-Attached Storage (NAS) appliance, a Storage-Area Network (SAN), or any of the various clustered storage solutions, the metrics you should monitor remain the same: disk consumption and disk I/O consumption. Tracking available disk space and the rate at which you're able to access that space is irrelevant to which hardware solution you end up choosing; you still need to track them both.

Logs and backup: The metacapacity issue

Backups and logs can consume large amounts of storage, and instituting requirements for them can be a large undertaking. Both backups and logs are part of any sane Business Continuity Plan (BCP) and Disaster Recovery (DR) procedure, so you'll need to factor in those requirements along with the core business requirements. Everyone needs a backup plan, but for how long do you maintain backup data? A week? A month? Forever? The answers to those questions will differ from site to site, application to application, and business to business.

For example, when archiving financial information, you may be under legal obligation to store data for a specific period of time to comply with federal regulations. On the other hand, some sites—particularly search engines—typically *maintain* their stored data (such as search logs) for shorter durations in an effort to preserve user privacy.

Storage for backups and log archiving entails identifying how much of each you must have readily available (outlined in your rentention/purge policies) versus how much you can archive off to cheaper (usually slower) hardware. There's nothing particularly special about planning for this type of storage, but it's quite often overlooked, as sites don't usually depend on logging and backups for critical guarantees of uptime. We'll discuss how you go about measuring for growing storage needs later in this chapter. In the next chapter, we'll explore the process of forecasting those needs.

Measuring loads on web servers

Web server capacity is application-specific. Generally speaking, web servers are considered frontend machines that accept users' requests, make calls to backend resources (such as databases) then use the results of those calls to generate responses. Some applications make simple and fast database queries; others make fewer, but more complex queries. Some websites serve mostly static pages, whereas others prepare mainly dynamic content. You'll use both system and application-level metrics to take a long view of the usage metrics, which will serve as the foundation for your capacity plan.

Capacity planning for web servers (static or dynamic) is peak-driven, and therefore elastic, unlike storage consumption. The servers consume a wide range of hardware resources over a daily period, and have a breaking point somewhere near the saturation of those resources. The goal is to discover the periodic peaks and use them to drive your capacity trajectory. As with any peak-driven resource, you'll want to find out when your peaks are, and then drill down into what's actually going on during those cycles.

A real-world example: Web server measurement

As an example, let's take a look at the hourly, daily, and weekly metrics of a single Apache web server. Figure 3-4 presents graphs of all three time frames, from which we'll try to pick out peak periods.

The hourly graph reveals no particular pattern, while the daily graph shows a smooth decline and rise. Most interesting in terms of capacity planning is the weekly graph, which indicates Mondays undergo the highest web server traffic. As the saying goes: X marks the spot, so let's start digging.

First, let's narrow down what hardware resources we're using. We can pare this list down further by ignoring resources that are operating well within their limits during peak time. Looking at memory, disk I/O, and network resources (not covered in this chapter), we can see none of them come close to approaching their limits during peak times. By eliminating those resources from the list of potential bottlenecks, we already know something significant about our web server capacity. What's left is CPU time, which we can assume is the critical resource. Figure 3-5 displays two graphs tracking CPU usage.

Figure 3-5 demonstrates that at peak, with user and system CPU usage combined, we're just a bit above 50 percent of total CPU capacity. Let's compare the trend with the actual work that is done by the web server so we can see whether the peak CPU usage has any visible effects on the application layer. Figure 3-6 shows the number of busy Apache processes at each unit of time we measure.

The graphs in Figures 3-5 and 3-6 confirm what you might expect: the number of busy Apache processes proportionally follows the CPU usage. Drilling into the most recent RRD values, at 50.7 percent of total CPU usage (45.20 user + 5.50 system), we're engaging 46 Apache processes. If we assume this relationship between CPU and busy Apache processes

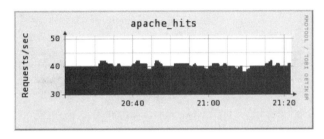

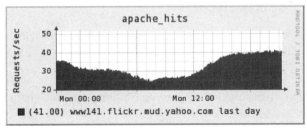

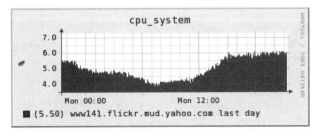

FIGURE 3-4. Hourly, daily, and weekly view of Apache requests

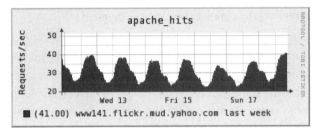

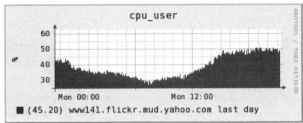

FIGURE 3-5. User and system CPU on a web server: daily view

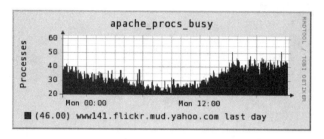

FIGURE 3-6. Busy Apache processes: daily view

stays the same—that is, if it's linear—until CPU usage reaches some high (and probably unsafe) value we haven't encountered in our graphs, we can have some reasonable confidence that our CPU capacity is adequate.

But hey, that's quite an assumption. Let's try to confirm it through another form of capacity planning: *controlled load testing*.

Finding web server ceilings in a load-balancing environment

Capturing the upper limit of your web server's resources can be simplified by at least one design decision that you've probably already made: using a load balancer. In order to confirm your ceiling estimates with live traffic, increase the production load carefully on some web servers and measure the effects it has on resources. Increase the load by pulling machines from the live pool of balanced servers, which increases the load on the remaining servers commensurately. I want to emphasize the importance of using real traffic instead of running a simulation or attempting to model your web server's resources in a benchmark-like setting.

Our artificially load-balanced exercise confirms the assumption we made in the previous section, which is: the relationship between CPU usage and busy Apache processes remain (roughly) constant. Figure 3-7 graphs the increase in active Apache processes and corresponding CPU usage.

This graph was generated from the RRDs produced by one of Flickr's web servers throughout its daily peaks and valleys, sorted by increasing amount of total CPU. It confirms CPU usage does indeed follow the number of busy Apache processes, at least between the values of 40 and 90 percent of CPU.

This suggests at Flickr we are safe using CPU as our single defining metric for capacity on our web servers. In addition, it directly correlates to the work done by the web server—and hopefully correlates further to the website's traffic. Using this information as a basis, we currently set our upper limit on total CPU to be 85 percent, which gives enough headroom to handle occasional spikes while still making efficient use of our servers.

A little more digging shows the ratio of CPU usage to busy Apache processes to be about 1.1, which allows us to compute one from the other. In general, finding a simple relationship between system resource statistics and application-level work will be valuable when you move on to forecasting usage.

PRODUCTION LOAD TESTING WITH A SINGLE MACHINE

When you have the luxury of using a load balancer to add and remove servers into production, it makes the task of finding capacity ceilings easy. But when you have only a single machine, things become somewhat more difficult. How can you increase load on that one machine?

You can't call the users and ask them to start clicking faster, but you can add load on your server by *replaying* requests you've seen in production. Many tools are available to do this, including two in particular with which I've had good experiences:

- Httperf (*http://www.hpl.hp.com/research/linux/httperf/*)
- Siege (*http://www.joedog.org/JoeDog/Siege*)

Both of these tools allow you to take a file filled with HTTP URLs and replay them at varying speeds against your server. This enables you to increase load very slowly and carefully, which is critical in a single-machine environment—you don't want to do any load testing that would kill your only running server. This not-very-safe technique should only be used to stretch the server's abilities a little at a time under safe conditions, such as during a low-traffic period.

Artificial load testing, even by replaying real production logs, brings with it a whole slew of limitations. Even though these tools give fine-grained control over the rate of requests, and you can control what requests are being made, they still don't accurately portray how your server will behave under duress.

For example, depending on how you allow your application to change data, simulating production loads with logs of previous requests can be difficult. You might not want to rewrite data you've already written, so you'll need to do some massaging of the logs you're replaying.

Another limitation is common to all web load-testing scenarios: an accurate representation of the client/server relationship. By using Httperf or Siege, you can simulate multiple clients, but in reality all the requests will be coming from a single client server that's running the script. A workaround for running these tools from a single machine is to run the scripts from multiple machines. A tool called Autobench (*http://www.xenoclast.org/autobench/*) is a Perl wrapper around Httperf that enables it to be run from multiple hosts in a coordinated fashion. Autobench can also aggregate the results for you.

But even Autobench, produces different results from real-world requests. Clients can be all over the globe, with wildly different network latencies, connection speeds, and many other variables.

Also be careful about cranking up the request rate from a single client machine. You might run out of client resources before you run out of server resources, which will further taint your results. Be sure to stay below the client's file descriptor maximums, network limits, and CPU limits during these artificial tests.

Instead of spending time working around the limitations of artificial testing, you should consider upgrading your architecture to make it easier to find your server's upper limits. A load balancer—even with just one extra server—not only helps you find limits but provides a more robust architecture overall.

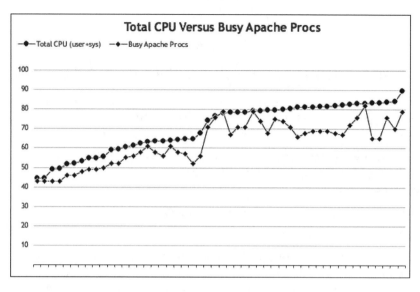

FIGURE 3-7. Total CPU versus busy Apache processes

Database Capacity

Nearly every dynamic website uses some form of a database to keep track of its data. This means you need to provide the capacity for it. In the LAMP world, MySQL and Postgres are favorite databases, while Oracle, Microsoft SQL server, and a myriad of others also serve as the backend data store for many successful sites.

Outside of the basic server statistics, there are a number of database-specific metrics you'll want to track:

- Queries-per-second (SELECTs, INSERTs, UPDATEs, and DELETEs)
- Connections currently open
- Lag time between master and slave during replication
- Cache hit rates

Planning the capacity needs of databases—particularly clusters of them—can be tricky business. Establishing the performance ceilings of your databases can be difficult because there might be hidden cliffs that only reveal themselves in certain edge cases.

For example, in the past we've made assumptions at Flickr that our databases running on a given hardware platform had a ceiling of X queries-per-second before performance began to degrade unacceptably. But we were surprised to learn that some queries perform fine on a user with fewer than 10,000 photos, but slow down alarmingly on a user who has more than 100,000 photos. (Yes, some Flickr users do upload hundreds of thousands of photos there!) So, we redefined our ceilings for the database server that handles users with large numbers of photos. This type of creative sleuthing of capacity and performance is mandatory with databases, and underscores the importance of understanding how the databases are actually being used outside the perspective of system statistics.

At this stage I'll reiterate my point about performance tuning. As pointed out in Jeremy Zawodny and Derek Balling's book, *High Performance MySQL*, database performance often depends more on your schemas and queries than on the speed of your hardware. Because of this, developers and database administrators focus on optimizing their schemas and queries, knowing that doing so can change the performance of the database quite dramatically. This in turn, affects your database ceilings. One day you think you need 10 database servers to get 20,000 queries-per-second; the next day you find you'll only need five, because you (or your programmers) were able to optimize some of the more common (or computationally expensive) queries.

A real-world example: Database measurement

Databases are complex beasts, and finding the limits of your database can be time consuming, but well worth the effort. Just as with web servers, database capacity tends to be peak-driven, meaning their limits are usually defined by how they perform during the heaviest periods of end-user activity. As a result, we generally take a close look at the peak traffic times to see what's going on with system resources, and take it from there.

But before we start hunting for the magical "red line" of database consumption, remember, I recommend looking at how your database performs with *real* queries and *real* data.

One of the first things you should determine is when your database is expected to run out of hardware resources, relative to traffic. Depending on the load characteristics, you might be bound by the CPU, the network, or disk I/O.

If you are lucky enough to keep your most-requested data in memory, you might find yourself being constrained by CPU or network resources. This situation makes your hunt for a performance ceiling a bit easier as you need only track a single number, as we discovered when monitoring Apache performance.

If your data is substantially larger than what you can fit into physical memory, your database's performance will be limited by the slowest piece of equipment: your physical disk. Because of the random nature of database-driven websites, queries for data on databases tend to be yet even more random, and the resulting disk I/O is correspondingly random. Random disk I/O tends to be slow, because the data being requested is bound by the disk's ability to seek back and forth to random points on the platter. Therefore, many growing websites eventually have disk I/O as their defining metric for database capacity.

As it turns out, our databases at Flickr are currently in that position. We know this by taking even a cursory look at our disk utilization statistics, in conjunction with the fact that the data requested from MySQL is much larger than the amount of physical memory we have. Let's use one of the servers as an example. Figure 3-8 shows the relevant MySQL metrics for a single Flickr user database during a peak hour.

Figure 3-8 depicts the rate of concurrent MySQL connections along with the rate of INSERTs, UPDATEs, DELETEs, and SELECTs per second for a single hour. There are a few spikes during this time in each of the metrics, but only one stands out as a potential item of interest.

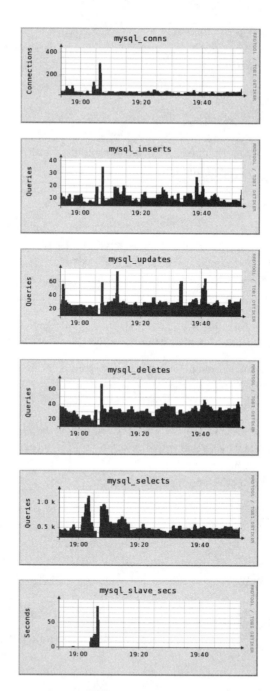

FIGURE 3-8. Production database MySQL metrics

The bottom graph shows the amount of database replication lag experienced during the last hour; it peaks at over 80 seconds. We don't like to see that degree of lag in database replication because it generally means the slaves temporarily lack a lot of the recent data loaded onto the master. Flickr directs all user queries to the slaves, which means until the slaves catch up to the master, users won't see the most up-to-date data. This can cause various unwelcome effects, such as a user annotating a photo, clicking the Submit button, but not seeing that comment right away. This is confusing for the user and can result in all sorts of out-of-sync weirdness. It's not ideal, to say the least.

From past experience, I'm aware our databases are disk I/O bound, but let's confirm that by taking a look at disk utilization and I/O wait in Figure 3-9.

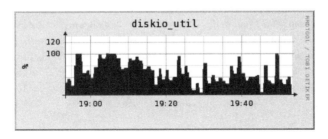

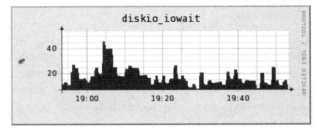

FIGURE 3-9. Production database disk utilization and I/O wait

In this example, we have Ganglia collecting and graphing disk utilization statistics for our database. These are reported every 60 seconds by some of the fields returned by the Linux *iostat* command, %iowait and %ioutil.

Note on the graph that while disk utilization jumped up to 100 percent more than once, it was only during the period where I/O wait bumped over the 40 percent mark that the MySQL replication lag jumped.

What does this mean? With nothing more than a cursory look at our metrics, we can deduce that replication slave lag is caused by disk I/O wait rather than disk utilization. We can further deduce that the replication lag becomes a problem only at a disk I/O wait of 40 percent or higher. Bear in mind these results apply only to a particular configuration at Flickr; this is an example rather than a general rule. The results make me wonder: could they indicate something defective with this particular server? Possibly, and the hypothesis should be easy enough to verify by provoking the behavior on similar production hardware. In this case, my examination of graphs from other servers demonstrates the relationship to be a general one that applies to Flickr activity at the time: other databases of identical hardware in production experience replication lag starting in, or near 40 percent disk I/O wait.

CURIOSITY KILLED THE CAPACITY PLAN

Let's take a moment to address a question that may have arisen in your mind: if the spike is not spe-cific to a hardware defect, and is indeed due to a legitimate database event, what is triggering it? This is a pertinent question, but its answer won't get you any further in assessing how many database servers you'll need to handle your traffic. There will always be spikes in resource usage, bugs, bad queries, and other unforeseen hiccups. Your job as a capacity planner is to take the bad with the good, and assume the bad won't go away. Of course, after you've submitted your hardware purchase justifications, by all means, don your performance-tuning hat and go after the cause of that spike with a vengeance. Indeed, finding the cause should be a mandatory next step, just don't let the investiga-tion of one anomaly get in the way of forecasting capacity needs.

Armed with these metrics, we now we have a degree of confidence the 40 percent disk I/O wait threshold is our ceiling for this database. As it relates to hardware configuration and our database query mix and rate, we should plan on staying below 40 percent disk I/O wait. But what does that mean in terms of actual database work?

Before we dig a bit further into the numbers, let's apply the same test method as we did with the web servers: increase production load on the database.

Finding database ceilings

A more focused and aggressive approach to finding database ceilings is to slowly (but again, carefully) increase the load on a live production server. If you maintain only a sin-gle database, this can be difficult to do safely. With only a single point of failure, testing runs the risk of bringing your site down entirely. This exercise becomes markedly easier if you employ any sort of database load balancing (via hardware appliance or within the application layer). In Figure 3-10, let's revisit the diagram of a common database architec-ture, this time with more real-world details added.

In this scenario, all database write operations are directed to the master; read functions are performed by database slaves. The slaves are kept up to date by replication. To pinpoint the ceilings of your database slaves, you want to increase the load on one of them by instructing your application to favor that particular device. If you operate a hardware load balancer for your databases, you may be able to weight one of the servers higher than the others in the balanced pool.

Increasing load to a database in this manner can reveal the effects load has on your resources, and hopefully expose the point at which your load will begin to affect replica-tion lag. In our case, we'd hope to confirm our educated guess of 40 percent disk I/O wait is the upper limit the database can withstand without inducing replication lag.

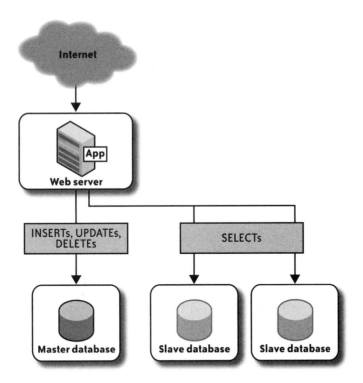

FIGURE 3-10. A master-slave database architecture

This example reflects a common database capacity issue defined by disk I/O. Your databases might be CPU-, memory-, or network-bound, but the process of finding the ceiling of each server is the same.

Caching Systems

We mentioned earlier that disks are the slowest pieces of your infrastructure, which makes accessing them expensive in terms of time. Most large-scale sites alleviate the need for making these expensive operations by caching data in various locations.

In web architectures, caches are most often used to store database results (as with Memcached) or actual files (as with Squid or Varnish). Both approaches call for the same considerations with respect to capacity planning. They are examples of *reverse proxies*, which are specialized systems that cache data sent from the web server to the client (usually a web browser).

First let's take a look at the diagram in Figure 3-11 to see how Squid and Varnish caching normally works with servers.

As Figure 3-12 shows, the diagram differs only slightly when illustrating database caching in the style of Memcached.

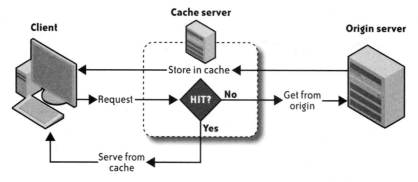

FIGURE 3-11. Basic content server caching mechanisms (reverse-proxy)

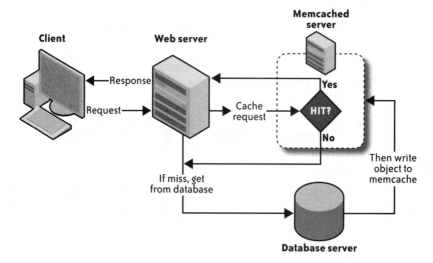

FIGURE 3-12. Database caching

Cache efficiency: Working sets and dynamic data

The two main factors affecting cache capacity are the size of your *working set* and the extent to which your data is dynamic or changing.

How often your data changes will dictate whether you'll choose to cache that data. On one end of the spectrum is data that almost never changes. Examples of this type of data include user names and account information. On the other end of the spectrum is information that changes frequently, such as the last comment made by a user, or the last photo uploaded. Figure 3-13 illustrates the relationship between caching efficiency and types of data.

It should be obvious there's no benefit in caching data that changes frequently, because the proxy will spend more time invalidating the cache than retrieving data from it. Every application will have its own unique characteristics with respect to caching, so there isn't any rule of thumb to follow. However, measuring and recording your cache's hit ratio is

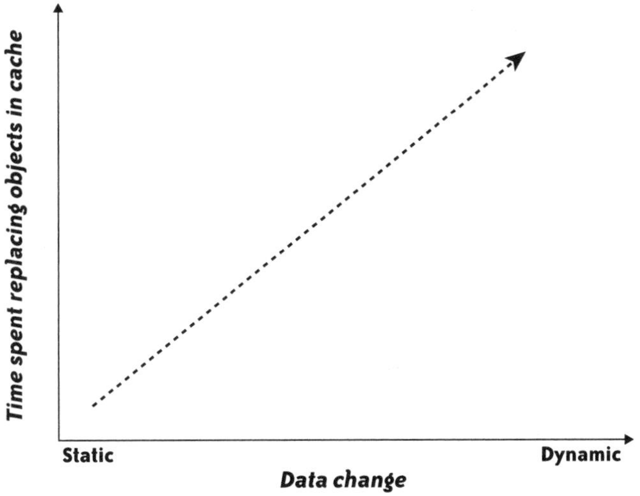
Time spent replacing objects in cache
Static
Dynamic
Data change

FIGURE 3-13. Cache efficiency depends on rate of change

imperative to understanding how efficient it is. This can help guide your capacity plan and hopefully steer how (and when) you'll want to cache objects.

The other major consideration is the size of your *working set* of cacheable objects. Caches have a fixed size. Your working set of cacheable objects is the number of unique objects—whether database results or files—requested over a given time period. Ideally, you'll have enough cache capacity to handle your entire working set. This would mean the vast majority of requests to the cache would result in cache hits. However, in real terms, there could be many reasons why you can't keep all the objects you want in cache. You would then need to depend on something called *cache eviction* to make room for new objects coming in. I'll present more on cache eviction later.

In order to function, caching software needs to keep track of its own metrics internally. Because of this, most proxies expose those metrics, allowing them to be measured and recorded by your monitoring tools.

At Flickr, we use Squid for reverse-proxy caching of photos. We use slower, cheaper, and larger capacity disks to store the photos, but we employ caching systems that use smaller and faster disks to serve those photos. We horizontally scale the number of caching servers as the request rate for photos increases. We also horizontally scale the backend persistent storage as the number of photos grows.

Each caching server has a limited amount of disk and memory available to use as cache. Because our working set of photos is too large to fit into our caches, the caches fill up. A full cache needs to constantly make decisions on which objects to evict to make room for new objects coming in. This process is based on a replacement or "eviction" algorithm. There are many eviction algorithms, but one of the most common is Least Recently Used (LRU), which is demonstrated in Figure 3-14.

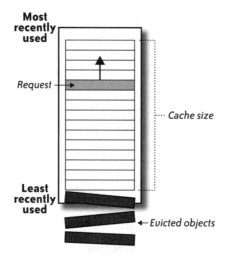

Most recently used

Request

Cache size

Least recently used

← Evicted objects

FIGURE 3-14. The LRU cache eviction algorithm

As requests come into a cache, the objects are organized into a list based on when each was last requested. A cache-missed object, once retrieved from the origin server, will be placed at the top of the list, and a cache hit will also be moved from its current location to the top of the list. This keeps all of the objects in order from most recently used to least recently used. When the cache needs to make room for new objects, it will remove objects from the bottom of the list. The age of the oldest object on the list is known as the *LRU reference age*, and is an indicator of how efficient the cache is, along with the hit ratio.

The LRU algorithm is used in Memcached, Squid, Varnish, and countless other caching applications. Its behavior is well known, and relatively simple to understand. Squid offers a choice of some more complex eviction algorithms, but nearly all of the most popular database caches use the LRU method.

The most important metrics to track with any caching software are:

- Cache hit ratio
- Total request rate
- Average object size
- LRU reference age (when using the LRU method)

Let's take a look at some caching metrics (compiled using Squid) from production.

Establishing Caching System Ceilings

The capacity of caching systems is defined differently depending on their usage. For a cache that can hold its entire working set, the request rate and response time might dictate its upper limits. In this case, you can again make use of the same method we applied to web serving and database disk I/O wait: carefully increase the load on a server in production, gather metric data along the way, and tie system resource metrics (CPU, disk I/O, network, memory usage) to the caching system metrics listed in the previous section.

Determining the ceiling of a cache when it is constantly full and must continually evict objects is a complicated exercise. It may better be defined not by request rate, but by its hit ratio (and indirectly, its reference age).

Table 3-2 summarizes cache planning considerations.

TABLE 3-2. Cache planning considerations

Type of cache use	Characteristics	Cache ceilings	Resource ceilings
Small, or slowly increasing working set	100% contained in cache	Request rate	Disk I/O utilization and wait, CPU and memory usage
Large, or growing working set	Moving window, constant eviction (churn)	Hit ratio, LRU reference age	Cache size

A real-world example: Cache measurement

As I mentioned earlier, at Flickr we need to take into account all of the metrics mentioned in the previous section. Our caches are constantly full, and cache eviction is a continuous process as users regularly upload new photos. We make use of Squid's memory and disk cache, so both of those resources need to be measured as well.

Let's first take a look at the graphs in Figure 3-15 to see what effect request rates are having on our system resources.

As you can see from the graphs, the Squid request rate increased steadily within the time period shown. The zigzag pattern represents the weekly peak activity periods (Mondays) we discovered earlier. For the same time period, the total CPU usage has increased as well, but we're not in any immediate danger of running out of CPU resources. Because we make extensive use of disk cache on our Squid servers, we'll want to take a look our disk I/O usage as well. See Figure 3-16 for the results.

Figure 3-16 confirms what we suspected: the amount of operations waiting for disk activity follows the rate of requests in near perfect synchronization. Since we know our Squid server uses the disk more than any other resource, such as CPU or memory, this tells us the defining peak resource metric is disk I/O wait—the same as our database ceiling. If we zoom into the data using RRDTool to overlay disk I/O wait and our request rate, we can plot them against each other in Excel, as shown in Figure 3-17.

Now that we have our correlation, let's sort the data in Excel as a function of increasing order and plot it again. As illustrated in Figure 3-18, this permits us to more easily see the trends related to the amount of the data requested at a particular moment.

Now we can clearly see how the two metrics relate to each other as they go up, and how disk I/O wait affects Squid's performance.

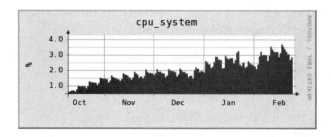

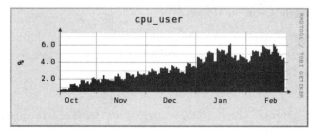

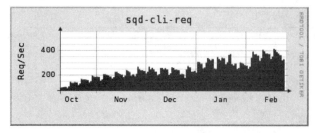

FIGURE 3-15. Five-month view of Squid request rate and CPU load (user and system)

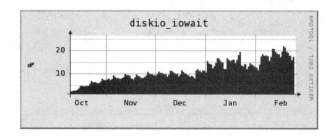

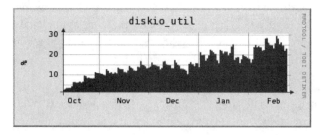

FIGURE 3-16. Five-month view of Squid server disk I/O wait and utilization

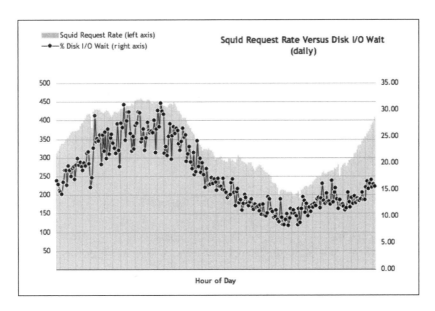

FIGURE 3-17. Squid request rate versus disk I/O wait: daily view

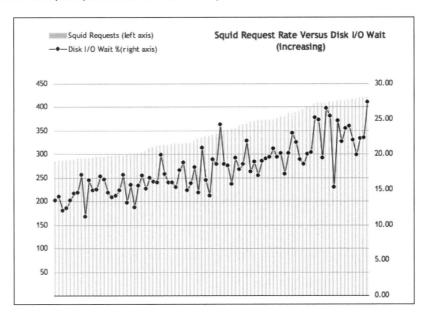

FIGURE 3-18. Squid request rate versus disk I/O wait: increasing view

Squid keeps internal metrics regarding the time it takes to handle both cache hits and misses. We can collect those metrics in Ganglia as well. We're not very concerned about the time spent for cache misses, because for the most part that doesn't inform us as to the upper limits of our cache—handling a miss mostly strains the network and origin server. Hits come from Squid's memory and disk cache, so that's where we want to focus our attention. Figure 3-19 presents the results over a five-month period.

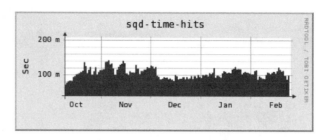

FIGURE 3-19. Squid hit time (in milliseconds): five-month view

This illustrates how the time for a cache hit has not changed significantly over the time period we're measuring (hovering around 100 milliseconds). Note that squid's "time-to-serve" metrics include the time until the client finishes receiving the last byte of the response, which can vary depending on how far your clients are from the server. This informs us that while disk I/O wait has increased, it has not affected the response time of the Squid server—at least not with the load it has been experiencing. We'd like to keep the time-to-serve metric within a reasonable range so the user isn't forced to wait for photos, so we've arbitrarily set a maximum time-to-serve of 180 milliseconds for this particular server; we'll still want to stay below that. But what amount of traffic *will* push our time-to-serve above that threshold?

In order to find that out, let's go to our stalwart load-increaser exercise. We'll want to increase production load slowly on the servers while recording their metrics. Since we now know which of our hardware resources follows increasing traffic, we know what to watch for: the threshold at which disk I/O wait starts to affect cache hit response time.

Increasing the request rate to our Squid server should be done slowly to avoid completely flooding our hit ratio. As depicted in Figure 3-20, by either replaying URLs via Httperf or Siege, or by removing servers from a load-balanced pool, we can bump up the request rate gradually on a single Squid server.

As you can see, the service time increases along with the disk I/O wait time (no surprise there). Due to a wide range of photo sizes, there's a lot of variation in our data for time-to-serve, but we begin to see 180 millisecond serving times at approximately 40 percent disk I/O wait. The only task remaining is to find the request rate at which we hit that threshold (see Figure 3-21).

Here, we see the "red line" we've been looking for (metaphorically speaking). At 40 percent disk I/O wait, we're processing upwards of 850 requests per second. If we use time-to-serve as a guide, this is going to be the maximum performance we can expect from our hardware platform with this particular configuration. As a point of reference, that configuration comprises a Dell PowerEdge 2950 with six 15,000 RPM SAS drives, 4 GB of RAM, and a single quad-core CPU.

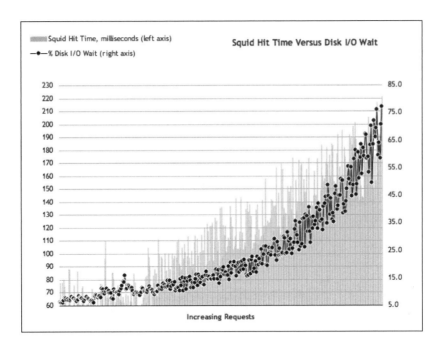

FIGURE 3-20. Testing for Squid ceilings: serving time versus disk I/O wait

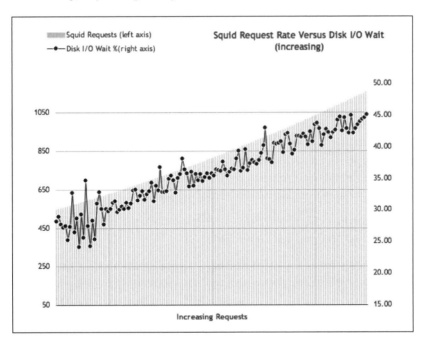

FIGURE 3-21. Squid request rate versus disk I/O wait, ceiling

However, we're not done with our cache measurements. We also need to confirm how our cache's efficiency changes over time, as we're handling a dynamic working set. Figure 3-22 presents the results from a five-month view.

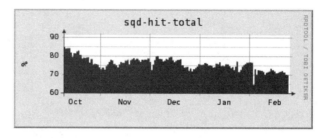

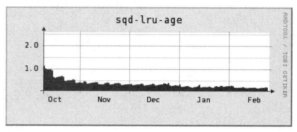

FIGURE 3-22. Cache hit ratios (%) and LRU age (days): five-month view

These two graphs display the hit ratio and LRU reference age of a particular Squid caching server we used to serve images over a period of five months. The hit ratio is expressed as a percentage, and the LRU reference age as units of days. During that time, LRU age and hit rate have both declined at a small but discernible rate, which we can attribute to the increase in photos being uploaded by users. As the working set of requested photos grows, the cache needs to work increasingly harder to evict objects to make room for new ones.

But even with this decrease in efficiency, it appears with a 72 percent hit rate, our LRU reference age for this server is about three hours. This is nothing to sneeze at, and is perfectly acceptable for our environment. We'll want to keep an eye on the hit rate as time goes on and continue to tune the cache size as appropriate.

To summarize, this exercise involved two metrics related to the ceilings experience by our caching system: disk I/O wait and cache efficiency.

As the request rate goes up, so does the demand on our disk subsystem and our time-to-serve. At roughly 850 requests per second, we can maintain what we deem to be an acceptable end-user experience. As we approach that number, we'll want to increase the number of cache servers to comfortably handle the load.

The ceiling of 850 requests per second assumes we have a steady cache hit ratio, which could also change over time.

Special Use and Multiple Use Servers

In our web server example, CPU usage was our defining metric. Admittedly, this makes the job pretty easy; you have a fixed amount of CPU to work with. It was also made less difficult by virtue of the fact Apache was the only significant application using the CPU. There are many circumstances though, in which you don't have the luxury of dedicating each server to do a single task. Having a server perform more than one task—email, web, uploads—can make more efficient use of your hardware, but it complicates taking measurements.

Our process thus far has been to tie system resources (CPU, memory, network, disk, and so on) to application-level metrics (Apache hits, database queries, etc.). When you run many different processes, it's difficult to track how their usage relates to each other, and how each process might signal it's reaching the upper limits of efficient operation.

But simply because this scenario can complicate capacity measurements, you need not assume it makes planning impossible.

In order to discern what processes are consuming which resources, you'll want to do one of the following:

- Isolate each running application and measure its resource consumption

- Hold some of the applications' resource usage constant in order to measure one at a time

The process requires some poking around in the data to find situations in which events just happen to run controlled experiments for you. For instance, as we'll see in the example later in this section, I happened to notice two days had similar web server traffic but different CPU usage. I could exploit this oddity to find out the constraints on capacity for the web server.

Once upon a time at Flickr, the photo upload and processing tasks resided on the same machines that were serving pages for the Flickr.com website; that configuration made capacity planning difficult. Image processing is a highly CPU-intensive task, and as the number of uploads increased, so did the dependence on disk I/O resources. Add to that the increase in our traffic, and we quickly discovered three different jobs were all fighting for the same resources.

At any given moment, we weren't exactly certain how much hardware was being used for each process, so we added some application-level metrics to guide our estimates:

- Photo uploads (which mostly drove disk I/O and network utilization)

- Image processing (which drove CPU utilization)

- Serving the site's pages (which drove both memory and CPU utilization)

I already knew our traffic pattern and shape for each of our system metrics, and now I could correlate them to the tasks they were doing. I wanted to isolate the resource effects of each of those tasks to track them separately, or at least get a good idea of what was doing what. Having these metrics already stored in RRD files, I could dump their values to text then load them into Excel, where I could conveniently graph them.

First I found a two-day period in which the pattern of web traffic was the similar for both days (Figure 3-23). At that time, the burden on our web servers included not only serving the site's page, but taking in photo uploads and processing them as well.

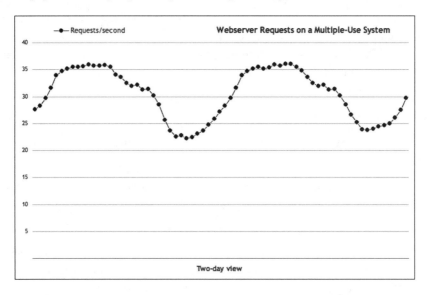

FIGURE 3-23. Two-day view of Apache requests

Now let's take a look at our system resources. In Figure 3-24, we have overlaid the CPU usage from Figure 3-23 onto the web server data for the same time period.

Clearly, the CPU was working harder on the second day, even though the amount of Apache traffic was roughly the same. The only other task this server was doing was image processing, so we know that we can attribute the different CPU usage to that image processing. What we want to do next is quantify that effect (see Figure 3-25).

This graph uncovers what we suspected: the extra CPU consumption on the second day was due to photo processing. This activity actually occurred over a weekend, and as we mentioned earlier in the chapter, Sundays are a high upload day.

Figure 3-26 plots the photo processing rates for both days against each other and shows the differences. Note that while the peaks for Sunday were more than 20 percent higher, during the evening the rate dropped below that of Saturday's rates at the same time, making the difference negative on the graph.

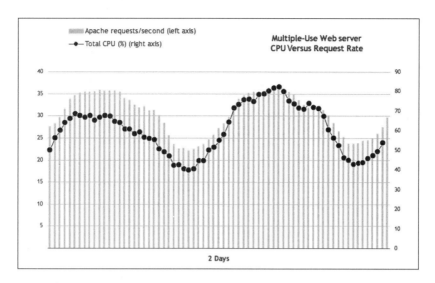

FIGURE 3-24. Web server work versus total CPU: two-day view

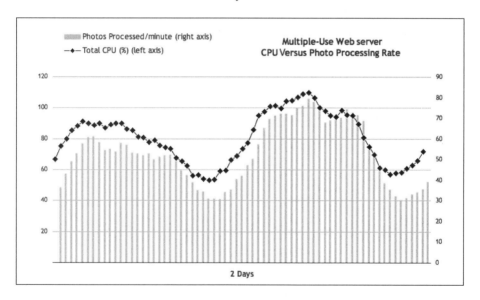

FIGURE 3-25. Total CPU versus photo processing rate, two-day view

We had all the data we needed to make an educated guess as to how much CPU is required to process images (as opposed to the amount required to serve Apache requests). We just needed to mine the data to come up with the specific values (Figure 3-27).

Figure 3-27 points out, at least for this given weekend, every 30 photos processed per minute can equate to an additional 25 percent CPU utilization.

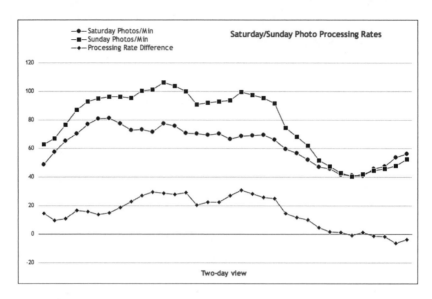

FIGURE 3-26. Saturday and Sunday photo processing rates

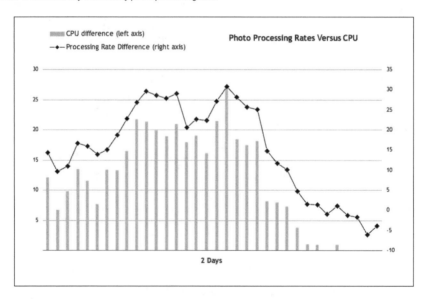

FIGURE 3-27. Photo processing rate and CPU usage, distilled from two-day data

This is an extremely rough estimate based on a small and statistically insignificant set of data, and you should consider this nothing more than an example of how to isolate resource usage on a multiple-use system. Confirming this 25:30 ratio using proper rigor would mean looking at a larger range of traffic and upload rates, and comparing the data again. But this process gives us a starting point from which we can base our ceilings.

In this situation, an ideal scenario is one in which we're tracking the two variables (web traffic and upload rates) and can figure out how many machines we'll need if we continue running both processes on each machine. This process worked for over a year in planning the capacity for Flickr's web servers. We finally split out the image processing onto its own dedicated cluster that could take advantage of multicore CPUs—another example of diagonal scaling at work.

API Usage and Its Effect on Capacity

As more and more websites use open APIs to open up their services to external developers, capacity planning for the use of those services must follow.

You may have guessed by now I'm a strong advocate of application-level metrics as well as system metrics, and API usage is the area where application-level metrics can matter the most. When you allow others access to your data via an open API, you're essentially allowing a much more focused and routine use of your website.

One of the advantages of having an open API is it allows for more efficient use of your application. If external developers wanted to gain access to your data and no API methods existed, they might *screen scrape* your site's pages to get at the data, which is extremely inefficient for a number of reasons. If they're only interested in a specific piece of data on the page, they'd still have to request the entire page and everything that entails, such as downloading CSS markup, JavaScript, and other components necessary for a client's browser to render the page, but of no interest to the developer. Although APIs allow more efficient use of your application, if not tracked properly, they also expose your web service to potential abuse, as they enable other applications to ask for those specific pieces of data.

Having some way to measure and record the usage of your open API on a per-user, or per-request-method basis, should be considered mandatory in capacity tracking on a site offering a web API. This is commonly done through the use of unique API *keys,* or other unique credentials. Upon each call to the API, the key identifies the application and the developer responsible for building the application.

Because it's much easier to issue an enormous volume of calls to an API than to use a regular client browser, you should keep track of what API calls are being made by what application, and at what rate.

At Flickr, we automatically invalidate any key that appears to be abusing the API, according to provisions outlined in the Terms of Service. We maintain a running total every hour for every API key that makes a call, how many calls were made, and the details of each call. See Figure 3-28 for the basic idea of API call metrics.

With this information, you can identify which API keys are responsible for the most traffic. You should be keeping track of the details of each key, as shown in Figure 3-29.

By collecting this information on a regular basis, you'll have a much better idea of how API usage affects your resources. You can then adjust API limits as your capacity landscape changes.

API Usage

Note: This is in UTC time. It is 8 hours ahead during daylight savings.

<<   Aug-07-2005   >>

Hourly Key Hits

5:59am - 6:59am	hits	avg hits/sec
Hourly total	18002	**5.00**

API Key

1745	3683	1.02
1236	2024	0.56
123	1427	0.40
321	1350	0.38
411	700	0.19
432	697	0.19
7899	638	0.18
2490	471	0.13
195	460	0.13
3555	410	0.11

FIGURE 3-28. Keeping track of API request statistics

Examples and Reality

Will *your* web servers, databases, storage, and caches exhibit the same behavior as these? It's almost guaranteed they won't because each application and type of data affects system resources differently. The examples in this chapter simply illustrate the methods and thought processes by which you can investigate and form a better understanding of how increased load can affect each part of your infrastructure.

The important lesson to retain is each segment of your architecture will spend system resources to serve your website, and you should make sure you're measuring those resources appropriately. However, recording the right measurements isn't enough. You need to have some idea of when those resources will run out, and that's why you periodically need to probe to establish those ceilings.

Running through the exercise of finding your architecture's upper limits can reveal bottlenecks you didn't even know existed. As a result, you might make changes to your application, your hardware, your network, or any other component responsible for the problem. Every time you make a change to your architecture, you'll need to check ceilings again, because they're likely to change. This shouldn't be a surprise, because by now you know that capacity planning is a process, not a one-time event.

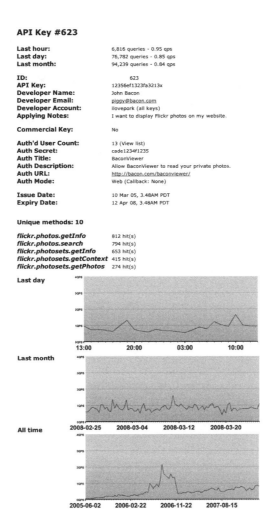

API Key #623

Last hour:	6,816 queries - 0.95 qps
Last day:	76,782 queries - 0.85 qps
Last month:	94,239 queries - 0.84 qps
ID:	623
API Key:	12356ef1323fa3213x
Developer Name:	John Bacon
Developer Email:	piggy@bacon.com
Developer Account:	ilovepork (all keys)
Applying Notes:	I want to display Flickr photos on my website.
Commercial Key:	No
Auth'd User Count:	13 (View list)
Auth Secret:	cade1234f1235
Auth Title:	BaconViewer
Auth Description:	Allow BaconViewer to read your private photos.
Auth URL:	http://bacon.com/baconviewer/
Auth Mode:	Web (Callback: None)
Issue Date:	10 Mar 05, 3.48AM PDT
Expiry Date:	12 Apr 08, 3.48AM PDT

Unique methods: 10

flickr.photos.getInfo	812 hit(s)
flickr.photos.search	794 hit(s)
flickr.photosets.getInfo	653 hit(s)
flickr.photosets.getContext	415 hit(s)
flickr.photosets.getPhotos	274 hit(s)

FIGURE 3-29. API key details and history

Summary

Measurement is a necessity, not an option. It should be viewed as the eyes and ears of your infrastructure. It can inform all parts of your organization: finance, customer care, engineering, and product management.

Capacity planning can't exist without the measurement and history of your system and application-level metrics. Planning is also ineffective without knowing your system's upper performance boundaries so you can avoid approaching them. Finding the ceilings of each part of your architecture involves the same process:

1. Measure and record the server's primary function.

   Examples: Apache hits, database queries

2. Measure and record the server's fundamental hardware resources.

   Examples: CPU, memory, disk, network usage

3. Determine how the server's primary function relates to its hardware resources.

   Examples: n database queries result in m percent CPU usage

4. Find the maximum acceptable resource usage (or ceiling) based on both the server's primary function and hardware resources by one of the following:

   - Artificially (and carefully) increasing real production load on the server through manipulated load balancing or application techniques.

   - Simulating as close as possible a real-world production load.

CHAPTER FOUR

Predicting Trends

I'M ASSUMING YOU'VE MADE A FEW PASSES THROUGH **CHAPTER 3** AND HAVE JUST DEPLOYED A SUPER-AWESOME, totally amazing, monitoring, trending, graphing, and measurement system. You're graphing everything you can get your hands on, as often as you can. You probably didn't gain anything from graphing the peak barking periods of your neighbor's dog—but hey, you did it, and I'm proud of you.

Now you'll be able to use this data (excluding the barking statistics) like a crystal ball, and predict the future like Nostradamus. But let's stop here for a moment to remember an irritating little detail: *it's impossible to accurately predict the future.*

Forecasting capacity needs is part intuition, and part math. It's also the art of slicing and dicing up your historical data, and making educated guesses about the future. Outside of those rare bursts and spikes of load on your system, the long-term view is hopefully one of steadily increasing usage. By putting all of this historical data into perspective, you can generate estimates for what you'll need to sustain the growth of your website. As we'll see later, the key to making accurate predictions is having an *adjustable* forecasting process.

DON'T BUY BEFORE YOU NEED IT

Before you get too excited about charting massive growth and putting new servers in place to handle the deluge, let me remind you of one of the key economic factors you need to deal with: buying equipment too early is wasteful.

This rule is derived directly from the obvious trend in computing costs: all forms of hardware are becoming cheaper, even as they become faster and more reliable. Whether or not Moore's Law (Gordon E. Moore's now-famous axiom in 1965 that postulates the number of transistors on an integrated circuit approximately doubles every eighteen months) holds true forever, we can predict that manufacturers will continue to lower costs over time. If you can wait six months before buying a piece of equipment, you will likely end up with faster and less expensive equipment at that time.

Certainly, you don't want to be caught unprepared when growth takes place—this book is all about saving you from that career-threatening situation. Conversely, the company financial officers will not hold you in high regard either when you've purchased a lot of equipment that lay idle, only to see its price drop a few months later.

Riding Your Waves

A good capacity plan depends on knowing your needs for your most important resources, and how those needs change over time. Once you have gathered historical data on capacity, you can begin analyzing it with an eye toward recognizing any trends and recurring patterns.

For example, in the last chapter I recounted how at Flickr, we discovered Sunday has been historically the highest photo upload day of the week. This is interesting for many reasons. It may also lead us to other questions: has that Sunday peak changed over time, and if so, how has it changed with respect to the other days of the week? Has the highest upload day always been Sunday? Does that change as we add new members residing on the other side of the International Date Line? Is Sunday still the highest upload day on holiday weekends? These questions can all be answered once you have the data, and the answers in turn could provide a wealth of insight with respect to planning new feature launches, operational outages, or maintenance windows.

Recognizing trends is valuable for many reasons, not just for capacity planning. When we looked at disk space consumption in Chapter 3, we stumbled upon some weekly upload patterns. Being aware of any recurring patterns can be invaluable when making decisions later on. Trends can also inform community management, customer care and support, product management, and finance. Some examples of how metrics measurement can be useful include:

- Your operations group can avoid scheduling maintenance that could affect image processing machines on a Sunday, opting for a Friday instead, to minimize any adverse effects on users.

- If you deploy any new code that touches the upload processing infrastructure, you might want to pay particular attention the following Sunday to see whether everything is holding up well when the system experiences its highest load.

- Making customer support aware of these peak patterns allows them to gauge the effect of any user feedback regarding uploads.

- Product management might want to launch new features based on the low or high traffic periods of the day. A good practice is to make sure everyone on your team knows where these metrics are located and what they mean.

- Your finance department might also want to know about these trends because it can help them plan for capital expenditure costs.

Trends, Curves, and Time

Let's take a look back at the daily storage consumption data we collected in the last chapter and apply it to make a forecast of future storage needs. We already know the defining metric: total available disk space. Graphing the cumulative total of this data provides the right perspective from which to predict future needs. Taking a look at Figure 4-1, we can see where we're headed with consumption, how it's changing over time, and when we're likely to run out of space.

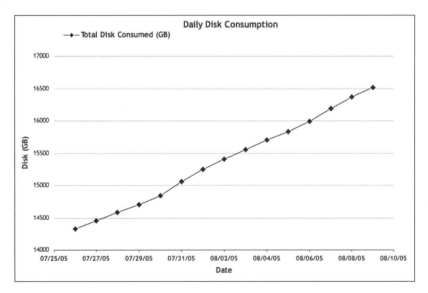

FIGURE 4-1. Total disk consumption: cumulative view

Now, let's add our constraint: the total currently available disk space. Let's assume for this example we have a total of 20 TB (or 20,480 GB) installed capacity. From the graph, we see we've consumed about 16 TB. Adding a solid line extending into the future to represent the total space we have installed, we obtain a graph that looks like Figure 4-2. This illustration demonstrates a fundamental principal of capacity planning: predictions require two essential bits of information, your ceilings and your historical data.

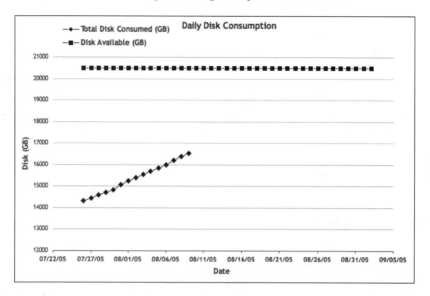

FIGURE 4-2. Cumulative disk consumption and available space

Determining when we're going to reach our space limitation is our next step. As I just suggested, we could simply draw a straight line that extends from our measured data to the point at which it intersects our current limit line. But is our growth actually linear? It may not be.

Excel calls this next step "adding a trend line," but some readers might know this process as *curve fitting*. This is the process by which you attempt to find a mathematical equation that mimics the data you're looking at. You can then use that equation to make educated guesses about missing values within the data. In this case, since our data is on a time line, the missing values in which we're interested are in the future. Finding a good equation to fit the data can be just as much art as science. Fortunately, Excel is one of many programs that feature curve fitting.

To display the trend using a more mathematical appearance, let's change the Chart Type in Excel from Line to XY (Scatter).

XY (Scatter) changes the date values to just single data points. We can then use the trending feature of Excel to show us how this trend looks at some point in the future. Right-click the data on the graph to display a drop-down menu. From that menu, select Add Trendline. A dialog box will open, as shown in Figure 4-3.

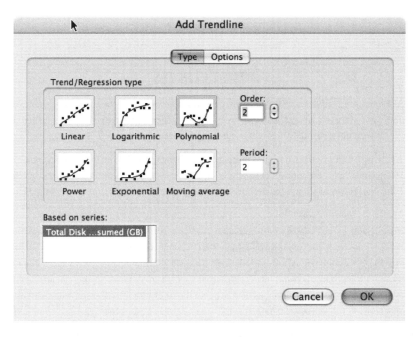

FIGURE 4-3. Add Trendline Type dialog box

Next, select a trend line type. For the time being, let's choose Polynomial, and set Order to 2. There may be good reasons to choose another trend type, depending on how variable your data is, how much data you have, and how far into the future you want to extrapolate. For more information, see the upcoming sidebar, "Fitting Curves."

In this example, the data appears about as linear as can be, but since I already know this data isn't linear over a longer period of time (it's accelerating), I'll pick a trend type that can capture some of the acceleration we know will occur.

After selecting a trend type, click the Options tab to bring up the Add Trendline options dialog box, as shown in Figure 4-4.

To show the equation that will be used to mimic our disk space data, click the checkbox for "Display equation on chart." We can also look at the R^2 value for this equation by clicking the "Display R-squared value on chart" checkbox.

The R^2 value is known in the world of statistics as the *coefficient of determination*. Without going into the details of how this is calculated, it's basically an indicator of how well an equation matches a certain set of data. An R^2 value of 1 indicates a mathematically perfect fit. With the data we're using for this example, any value above 0.85 should be sufficient. The important thing to know is, as your R^2 value decreases, so too should your confidence in the forecasts. Changing the trend type in the previous step affects the R^2 values—sometimes for better, sometimes for worse—so some experimentation is needed here when looking at different sets of data.

FITTING CURVES

In capacity planning, curve fitting is where the creative can collide with the scientific. In most cases, capacity planning is used to stay ahead of growth, which is generally represented through time-series data that extends upward and to the right in some form or manner.

Figuring out how and when the data gets there is the challenge, and we aim to use *extrapolation* to solve it. Extrapolation is the process of constructing new data points beyond a set of known data points. In our case, we're going to be defining new data points that exist in the future of time-series data.

The difficulty with curve fitting and extrapolation is you need to reconcile what you know about the source of your data with the apparent best-fit equation. Simply because you find a curve that fits the data with 99.999% mathematical accuracy doesn't mean it's going to be an accurate picture of the future. Your data will almost always have context outside of the mathematical equation. For example, forecasting the sale of snow shovels must include considerations for time of year (winter versus summer) or geography (Alaska or Arizona).

When finding equations to fit your data, it's also best to stay away from higher-order polynomial equations. They're tempting because their fit (*coefficient of determination*) is so good, but anything higher than a 2nd order polynomial can exhibit dramatic fluctuations outside of the dataset you're looking at.

The moral of the story is to use a good deal of common sense when curve-fitting your data. Don't insist on elegantly perfect fits, as they are quite often the result of questionable assumptions.

We'll want to extend our trend line into the future, of course. We want to extend it far enough into the future such that it intersects the line corresponding to our total available space. This is the point at which we can predict we'll run out of space. Under the Forecast portion of the dialog box, enter 25 units for a value. Our units in this case are days. After you hit OK, you'll see our forecast looks similar to Figure 4-5.

The graph indicates that somewhere around day 37, we run out of disk space. Luckily, we don't need to squint at the graph to see the actual values; we have the equation used to plot that trend line. As detailed in Table 4-1, plugging the equation into Excel, and using the day units for the values of X, we find the last day we're below our disk space limit is 8/30/05.

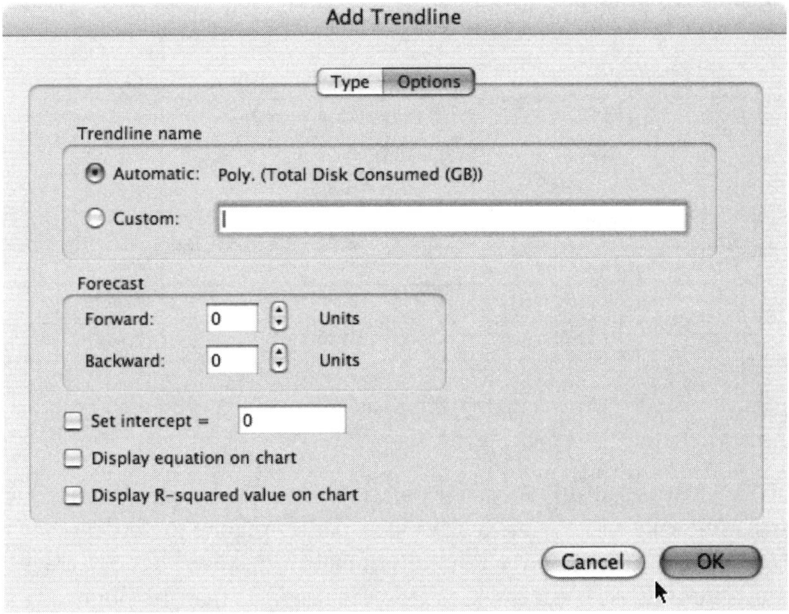

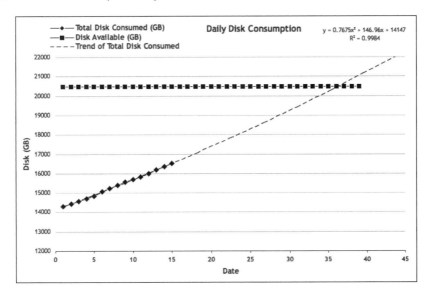

FIGURE 4-4. Add Trendline Options dialog box

FIGURE 4-5. Extending the trend line

	Date	Disk available (GB)	y=0.7675x2 + 146.96x + 14147
33	08/27/05	20480.00	19832.49
34	08/28/05	20480.00	20030.87
35	08/29/05	20480.00	20230.79
36	08/30/05	20480.00	20432.24
37	08/31/05	20480.00	20635.23
38	09/01/05	20480.00	20839.75
39	09/02/05	20480.00	21045.81

Now we know when we'll need more disk space, and we can get on with ordering and deploying it.

This example of increasing disk space is about as simple as they come. But as the metric is consumption-driven, every day has a new value that contributes to the definition of our curve. We also need to factor in the peak-driven metrics that drive our capacity needs in other parts of our site. Peak-driven metrics involve resources that are continually regenerated, such as CPU time and network bandwidth. They fluctuate more dramatically and thus are more difficult to predict, so curve fitting requires more care.

Tying Application Level Metrics to System Statistics: Database Example

In Chapter 3, we went through the exercise of establishing our database ceiling values. We discovered (through observing our system metrics) that 40 percent disk I/O wait was a critical value to avoid, because it's the threshold at which database replication begins experiencing disruptive lags.

How do we know when we'll reach this threshold? We need some indication when we are approaching our ceiling. It appears the graphs don't show a clear and smooth line just bumping over the 40 percent threshold. Instead, our disk I/O wait graph shows our database doing fine until a 40 percent spike occurs. We might deem occasional (and recoverable) spikes to be acceptable, but we need to track how our average values change over time so the spikes aren't so close to our ceiling. We also need to somehow tie I/O wait times to our database usage, and ultimately, what that means in terms of actual application usage.

To establish some control over this unruly data, let's take a step back from the system statistics and look at the purpose this database is actually serving. In this example, we're looking at a *user* database. This is a server in our main database cluster, wherein a segment of Flickr users store the metadata associated with their user account: their photos, their tags, the groups they belong to, and more. The two main drivers of load on the databases are, of course, the number of photos and the number of users.

This particular database has roughly 256,000 users and 23 million photos. Over time, we realized that neither the number of users nor the number of photos is singularly responsible for how much work the database does. Taking only one of those variables into account meant ignoring the effect of the other. Indeed, there may be many users who have few, or no photos; queries for their data is quite fast and not at all taxing. On the flip side, there are a handful of users who maintain enormous collections of photos.

We can look at our metrics for clues on our critical values. We have all our system metrics, our application metrics, and the historical growth of each.

We then set out to find the single most important metric that can define the ceiling for each database server. After looking at the disk I/O wait metric for each one, we were unable to distinguish a good correlation between I/O wait and the number of users on the database. We had some servers with over 450,000 users that were seeing healthy, but not dangerous, levels of I/O wait. Meanwhile, other servers with only 300,000 users were experiencing much higher levels of I/O wait. Looking at the number of photos wasn't helpful either—disk I/O wait didn't appear to be tied to photo population.

As it turns out, the metric that directly indicates disk I/O wait is the ratio of *photos-to-users* on each of the databases.

As part of our application-level dashboard, we measure on a daily basis (collected each night) how many users are stored on each database along with the number of photos associated with each user. The photos-to-user ratio is simply the total number of photos divided by the number of users. While this could be thought of as an average photos *per* user, the range can be quite large, with some "power" Flickr users having many thousands of photos while a majority have only tens or hundreds. By looking at how the *peak* disk I/O wait changes with respect to this photos per user ratio, we can get an idea of what sort of application-level metrics can be used to predict and control the use of our capacity (see Figure 4-6).

This graph was compiled from a number of our databases, and displays the peak disk I/O wait values against their current photos-to-user ratios. With this graph, we can ascertain where disk I/O wait begins to jump up. There's an elbow in our data around the 85–90 ratio when the amount of disk I/O wait jumps above the 30 percent range. Since our ceiling value is 40 percent, we'll want to ensure we keep our photos-to-user ratio in the 80–100 range. We can control this ratio within our application by distributing photos for high-volume users across many databases.

I want to stop here for a moment to talk a bit about Flickr's database architecture. After reaching the limits of the more traditional Master/Slaves MySQL replication architecture (in which all writes go to the master and all reads go to the slaves), we redesigned our database layout to be *federated*, or *sharded*. This evolution in architecture is becoming increasingly common as site growth reaches higher levels of changing data. I won't go into how that architectural migration came about, but it's a good example of how architecture decisions can have a positive effect on capacity planning and deployment. By federating our data across many servers, we limit our growth only by the amount of hardware we can deploy, not by the limits imposed by any single machine.

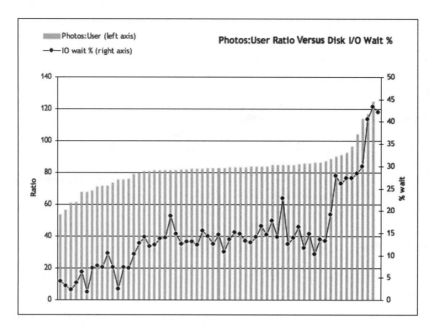

FIGURE 4-6. Database—photo:user ratio versus disk I/O wait percent

Because we're federated, we can control how users (and their photos) are spread across many databases. This essentially means each server (or pair of servers, for redundancy) contains a unique set of data. This is in contrast to the more traditional monolithic database that contains every record on a single server. More information about federated database architectures can be found in Cal Henderson's book, *Building Scalable Web Sites* (O'Reilly).

OK, enough diversions—let's get back to our database capacity example and summarize where we are to this point. Database replication lag is bad and we want to avoid it. We hit replication lag when we see 40 percent disk I/O wait, and we reach that threshold when we've installed enough users and photos to produce a photos-to-user ratio of 110. We know how our photo uploads and user registrations grow, because we capture that on a daily basis (Figure 4-7). We are now armed with all the information we need to make informed decisions regarding how much database hardware to buy, and when.

We can extrapolate a trend based on this data to predict how many users and photos we'll have on Flickr for the foreseeable future, then use that to gauge how our photos/user ratio will look on our databases, and whether we need to adjust the maximum amounts of users and photos to ensure an even balance across those databases.

We've found where the elbow in our performance (Figure 4-6) exists for these databases—and therefore our capacity—but what is so special about this photos/users ratio for our databases? Why does this particular value trigger performance degradation? It could be for many reasons, such as specific hardware configurations, or the types of queries that result from having that much data during peak traffic. Investigating the answers to these

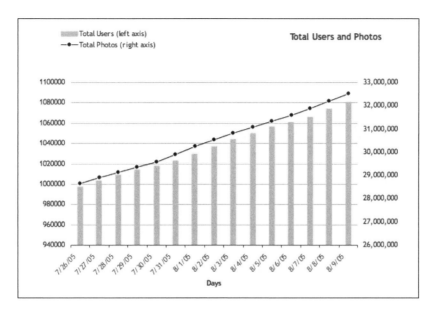

FIGURE 4-7. Photos uploaded and user registrations

questions could be a worthwhile exercise, but here again I'll emphasize that we should simply expect this effect will continue and not count on any potential future optimizations.

Forecasting Peak-Driven Resource Usage: Web Server Example

When we forecast the capacity of a peak-driven resource, we need to track how the peaks change over time. From there, we can extrapolate from that data to predict future needs. Our web server example is a good opportunity to illustrate this process.

In Chapter 3, we identified our web server ceilings as 85 percent CPU usage for this particular hardware platform. We also confirmed CPU usage is directly correlated to the amount of work Apache is doing to serve web pages. Also as a result of our work in Chapter 3, we should be familiar with what a typical week looks like across Flickr's entire web server cluster. Figure 4-8 illustrates the peaks and valleys over the course of one week.

This data is extracted from a time in Flickr's history when we had 15 web servers. Let's suppose this data is taken today, and we have no idea how our activity will look in the future. We can assume the observations we made in the previous chapter are accurate with respect to how CPU usage and the number of busy apache processes relate—which turns out to be a simple multiplier: 1.1. If for some reason this assumption *does* change, we'll know quickly, as we're tracking these metrics on a per-minute basis. According to the graph in Figure 4-8, we're seeing about 900 busy concurrent Apache processes during peak periods, load balanced across 15 web servers. That works out to about 60 processes per web server. Thus, each web server is using approximately 66 percent total CPU (we can look at our CPU graphs to confirm this assumption).

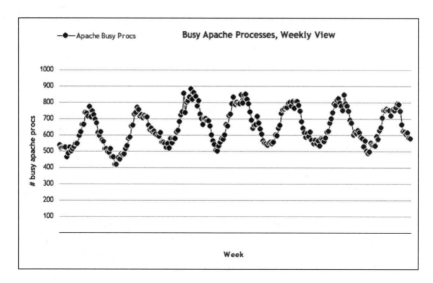

FIGURE 4-8. Busy Apache processes: weekly view

The peaks for this sample data are what we're interested in the most. Figure 4-9 presents this data over a longer time frame, in which we see these patterns repeat.

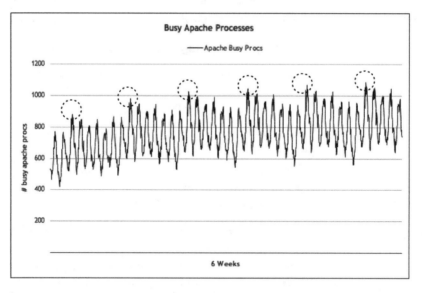

FIGURE 4-9. Weekly web server peaks across six weeks

It's these weekly peaks that we want to track and use to predict our future needs. As it turns out, for Flickr, those weekly peaks almost always fall on a Monday. If we isolate those peak values and pull a trend line into the future as we did with our disk storage example above, we'll see something similar to Figure 4-10.

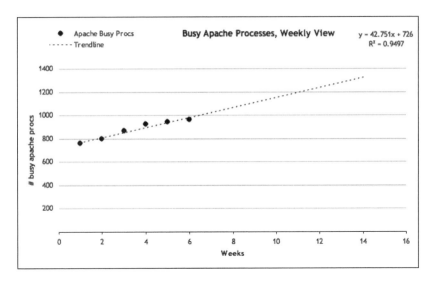

FIGURE 4-10. Web server peak trend

If our traffic continues to increase at the current pace, this graph predicts in another eight weeks, we can expect to experience roughly 1,300 busy Apache processes running at peak. With our 1.1 processes-to-CPU ratio, this translates to around 1,430 percent total CPU usage across our cluster. If we have defined 85 percent on each server as our upper limit, we would need 16.8 servers to handle the load. Of course, manufacturers are reluctant to sell servers in increments of tenths, so we'll round that up to 17 servers. We currently have 15 servers, so we'll need to add 2 more.

The next question is, when should we add them? As I explained in the sidebar "Don't Buy Before You Need It," we can waste a considerable amount of money if we add hardware too soon.

Fortunately, we already have enough data to calculate *when* we'll run out of web server capacity. We have 15 servers, each currently operating at 66 percent CPU usage at peak. Our upper limit on web servers is set at 85 percent, which would mean 1,275% CPU usage across the cluster. Applying our 1.1 multiplier factor, this in turn would mean 1,160 busy Apache processes at peak. If we trust the trend line shown in Figure 4-11, we can expect to run out of capacity sometime between the 9th and 10th week.

Therefore, the summary of our forecast can be presented succinctly:

- We'll run out of web server capacity three to four weeks from now.

- We'll need two more web servers to handle the load we expect to see in eight weeks.

Now we can begin our procurement process with detailed justifications based on hardware usage trends, not simply a wild guess. We'll want to ensure the new servers are in place before we need them, so we'll need to find out how long it will take to purchase, deliver, and install them.

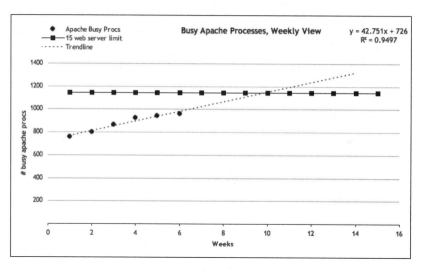

FIGURE 4-11. Capacity of 15 web servers

This is a simplified example. Adding two web servers in three to four weeks shouldn't be too difficult or stressful. Ideally, you should have more than six data points upon which to base your forecast, and you likely won't be so close to your cluster's ceiling as in our example. But no matter how much capacity you'll need to add, or how long the time-frame actually is, the process should be the same.

Caveats Concerning Small Data Sets

When you're forecasting with peak values as we've done, it's important to remember the more data you have to fit a curve, the more accurate your forecast will be. In our example, we based our hardware justifications on six weeks worth of data. Is that enough data to constitute a trend? Possibly, but the time period on which you're basing your forecasts is of great importance as well. Maybe there is a seasonal lull or peak in traffic, and you're on the cusp of one. Maybe you're about to launch a new feature that will add extra load to the web servers within the timeframe of this forecast. These are only a few considerations for which you may need to compensate when you're making justifications to buy new hardware. A lot of variables can come into play when predicting the future, and as a result, we have to remember to treat our forecasts as what they really are: educated guesses that need constant refinement.

Automating the Forecasting

Our use of Excel in the previous examples was pretty straightforward. But you can automate that process by using Excel macros. And since you'll most likely be doing the same process repeatedly as your metric collection system churns out new usage data, you can benefit greatly by introducing some automation into this curve-fitting business. Other benefits can include the ability to integrate these forecasts into a dashboard, plug them into other spreadsheets, or put them into a database.

An open source program called *fityk* (*http://fityk.sourceforge.net*) does a great job of curve-fitting equations to arbitrary data, and can handle the same range of equation types as Excel. For our purposes, the full curve-fitting abilities of fityk are a distinct overkill. It was created for analyzing scientific data that can represent wildly dynamic datasets, not just growing and decaying data. While fityk is primarily a GUI-based application (see Figure 4-12), a command-line version is also available, called *cfityk*. This version accepts commands that mimic what would have been done with the GUI, so it can be used to automate the curve fitting and forecasting.

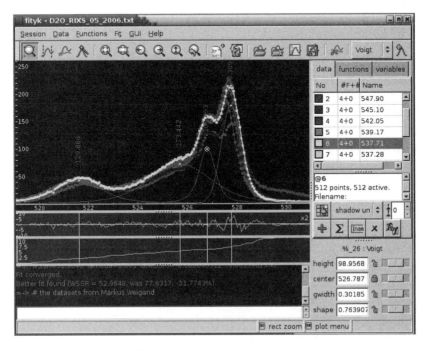

FIGURE 4-12. The fityk curve-fitting GUI tool

The command file used by cfityk is nothing more than a script of actions you can write using the GUI version. Once you have the procedure choreographed in the GUI, you'll be able to replay the sequence with different data via the command-line tool.

If you have a carriage return–delimited file of x-y data, you can feed it into a command script that can be processed by cfityk. The syntax of the command file is relatively straight-forward, particularly for our simple case. Let's go back to our storage consumption data for an example.

In the code example that follows, we have disk consumption data for a 15-day period, presented in increments of one data point per day. This data is in a file called *storage-consumption.xy*, and appears as displayed here:

```
1 14321.83119
2 14452.60193
3 14586.54003
```

```
 4 14700.89417
 5 14845.72223
 6 15063.99681
 7 15250.21164
 8 15403.82607
 9 15558.81815
10 15702.35007
11 15835.76298
12 15986.55395
13 16189.27423
14 16367.88211
15 16519.57105
```

The cfityk command file containing our sequence of actions to run a fit (generated using the GUI) is called *fit-storage.fit,* and appears as shown below:

```
# Fityk script. Fityk version: 0.8.2
@0 < '/home/jallspaw/storage-consumption.xy'
 guess Quadratic
 fit
info formula in @0
quit
```

This script imports our x-y data file, sets the equation type to a second-order polynomial (quadratic equation), fits the data, and then returns back information about the fit, such as the formula used. Running the script gives us these results:

```
jallspaw:~]$cfityk ./fit-storage.fit
1> # Fityk script. Fityk version: 0.8.2
2>  @0 < '/home/jallspaw/storage-consumption.xy'
15 points. No explicit std. dev. Set as sqrt(y)
3>  guess Quadratic
New function %_1 was created.
4>  fit
Initial values:  lambda=0.001  WSSR=464.564
#1:  WSSR=0.90162  lambda=0.0001  d(WSSR)=-463.663  (99.8059%)
#2:  WSSR=0.736787  lambda=1e-05  d(WSSR)=-0.164833  (18.2818%)
#3:  WSSR=0.736763  lambda=1e-06  d(WSSR)=-2.45151e-05  (0.00332729%)
#4:  WSSR=0.736763  lambda=1e-07  d(WSSR)=-3.84524e-11  (5.21909e-09%)
Fit converged.
Better fit found (WSSR = 0.736763, was 464.564, -99.8414%).
5> info formula in @0
# storage-consumption
14147.4+146.657*x+0.786854*x^2
6> quit
```

bye...

We now have our formula to fit the data:

$$0.786854x^2 + 146.657x + 14147.4$$

Note how the result looks almost exactly as Excel's for the same type of curve. Treating the values for *x* as days and those for *y* as our increasing disk space, we can plug in our 25-day forecast, which yields the same results as the Excel exercise. Table 4-2 lists the results generated by cfityk.

TABLE 4-2. Same forecast as Table 4-1, curve-fit by cfityk

	Date	Disk Available (GB)	$y=0.786854x^2 + 146.657x + 14147.4$
33	08/27/05	20480.00	19843.97
34	08/28/05	20480.00	20043.34
35	08/29/05	20480.00	20244.29
36	08/30/05	20480.00	20446.81
37	08/31/05	20480.00	20650.91
38	09/01/05	20480.00	20856.58
39	09/02/05	20480.00	21063.83

Being able to perform curve-fitting with a cfityk script allows you to carry out forecasting on a daily or weekly basis within a cron job, and can be an essential building block for a capacity planning dashboard.

Safety Factors

Web capacity planning can borrow a few useful strategies from the older and better-researched work of mechanical, manufacturing, and structural engineering. These disciplines also need to base design and management considerations around resources and immutable limits. The design and construction of buildings, bridges, and automobiles obviously requires some intimate knowledge of the strength and durability of materials, the loads each component is expected to bear, and what their ultimate failure points are. Does this sound familiar? It should, because capacity planning for web operations shares many of those same considerations and concepts.

Under load, materials such as steel and concrete undergo physical stresses. Some have elastic properties that allow them to recover under light amounts of load, but fail under higher strains. The same concerns exist in your servers, network, or storage. When their resources reach certain critical levels—100 percent CPU or disk usage, for example—they fail. To pre-empt this failure, engineers apply what is known as a *factor of safety* to their design. Defined briefly, a factor of safety indicates some margin of resource allocated beyond the theoretical capacity of that resource, to allow for uncertainty in the usage.

While safety factors in the case of mechanical or structural engineering are usually part of the design phase, in web operations they should be considered as an amount of available resources that you leave aside, with respect to the ceilings you've established for each class of resource. This will enable those resources to absorb some amount of unexpected increased usage. Resources with which you should calculate safety factors include all the those discussed in Chapter 3: CPU, disk, memory, network bandwidth, even entire hosts (if you run a very large site).

For example, in Chapter 3 we stipulated 85 percent CPU usage as our upper limit for web servers, in order to reserve "enough headroom to handle occasional spikes." In this case, we're allowing a 15 percent margin of "safety." When making forecasts, we need to take these safety factors into account and adjust the ceiling values appropriately.

Why a 15 percent margin? Why not 10 or 20 percent? Your safety factor is going to be somewhat of a slippery number or educated guess. Some resources, such as caching systems, can also tolerate spikes better than others, so you may want to be less conservative with a margin of safety. You should base your safety margins on "spikes" of usage that you've seen in the past. See Figure 4-13.

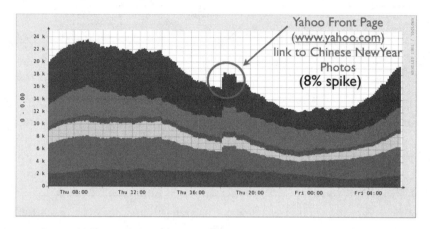

FIGURE 4-13. Spike in traffic from Yahoo Front Page

Figure 4-13 displays the effect of a typically-sized traffic spike Flickr experiences on a regular basis. It's by no means the largest. Spikes such as this one almost always occur when the front page of *http://www.yahoo.com* posts a prominent link to a group, a photo, or a tag search page on Flickr. This particular spike was fleeting; it lasted only about two hours while the link was up. It caused an eight percent bump in traffic to our photo servers. Seeing a 5–15 percent increase in traffic like this is quite common, and confirms that our 15 percent margin of safety is adequate.

Procurement

As we've demonstrated, with our resource ceilings pinpointed, we can predict when we'll need more of a particular resource. When we complete the task of predicting when we'll need more, we can use that timeline to gauge when to trigger the procurement process.

Your procurement pipeline is the process by which you obtain new capacity. It's usually the time it takes to justify, order, purchase, install, test, and deploy any new capacity. Figure 4-14 illustrates the procurement pipeline.

The tasks outlined in Figure 4-14 vary from one organization to another. In some large organizations, it can take a long time to gain approvals to buy hardware, but delivery can happen quickly. In a startup, approvals may come quickly, but the installation likely proceeds more slowly. Each situation will be different, but the challenge will remain the same: estimate how long the entire process will take, and add some amount of comfortable buffer to account for unforeseen problems. Once you have an idea of what that buffer timeline is, you can then work backward to plan capacity.

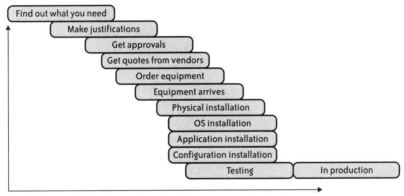

Time to production

FIGURE 4-14. Typical procurement pipeline

In our disk storage consumption example, we have current data on our disk consumption up to 8/15/05, and we estimate we'll run out of space on 8/30/05. You now know you have exactly two weeks to justify, order, receive, install, and deploy new storage. If you don't, you'll run out of space and be forced to trim that consumption in some way. Ideally, this two-week deadline will be long enough for you to bring new capacity online.

Procurement Time: The Killer Metric

Obviously, the *when* of ordering equipment is just as important as the *what* and *how much*. Procurement timelines outlined above hint at how critical it is to keep your eye on how long it will take to get what you need into production. Sometimes external influences, such as vendor delivery times and physical installation at the data center can ruin what started out to be a perfectly timed integration of new capacity.

Startups routinely order servers purely out of the fear they'll be needed. Most newly launched companies have developers to work on the product and don't need to waste money on operations-focused engineers. The developers writing the code are most likely the same people setting up network switches, managing user accounts, installing software, and wearing whatever other hats are necessary to get their company rolling. The last thing they want to worry about is running out of servers when they launch their new, awesome website. Ordering more servers as needed can be rightly justified in these cases, because the hardware costs are more than offset by the costs of preparing a more streamlined and detailed capacity plan.

But as companies mature, optimizations begin to creep in. Code becomes more refined. The product becomes more defined. Marketing starts to realize who their users are. The same holds true for the capacity management process; it becomes more polished and accurate over time.

Just-In-Time Inventory

Toyota Motors developed the first implementations of a just-in-time inventory practice. It knew there were large costs involved to organize, store, and track excess inventory of automobile parts, so it decided to reduce that "holding" inventory and determine exactly when it needed parts. Having inventory meant wasting money. Instead of maintaining a massive warehouse filled with the thousands of parts to make its cars, Toyota would only order and stock those parts as they were needed. This reduced costs tremendously and gave Toyota a competitive advantage in the 1950s. Just-in-time inventory practice is now part of any modern manufacturing effort.

The costs associated with having auto parts lying around in a warehouse can be seen analogous to having servers installed before you *really* need them. Rack space and power consumption in a data center cost money, as does the time spent installing and deploying code on the servers. More important, you risk suffering economically as a result of the aforementioned Moore's Law, which if your forecasts allow it, should motivate you to buy equipment later, rather than sooner.

Once you know when your current capacity will top out, and how much capacity you'll need to get through to the next cycle of procurement, you should take a few lessons from the just-in-time inventory playbook, whose sole purpose it is to eliminate waste of time and money in the process.

Here are some of the steps in our typical procurement process you'll want to pay attention to, and streamline:

1. Determine your needs

   You know how much load your current capacity can handle, because you've followed the advice in Chapter 3 to find their ceilings and are measuring their usage constantly. Take these numbers to the curve-fitting table and start making crystal ball predictions. This is fundamental to the capacity planning process.

2. Justify purchases

   Add some color and use attention-grabbing fonts on the graphs you just made in the previous step, because you're going to show them to the people who will approve the hardware purchases you're about to make. Spend as much time as you need to ensure your money-handling audience understands why you're asking for capacity, why you're asking for it now, and why you'll be coming back later asking for more. Be very clear in your presentations about the downsides of insufficient capacity.

3. Solicit quotes from vendors

   Vendors want to sell you servers and storage; you want to buy servers and storage—all is balanced in the universe. Why would you choose vendor A over vendor B? Because vendor A might help alleviate some of the fear normally associated with ordering servers, through such practices as quick turnarounds on quotes and replacements, discounts on servers ordered later, or discounts tied to delivery times.

4. Order equipment

   Can you track your order online? Do you have the phone number (gasp!) of a reliable human who can tell you where your equipment is at all times? Does the data center know the machines are coming, and have they factored that into their schedule?

5. Physical installation

   How long will it take for the machines to make the journey from a loading dock into a rack, and cabled up to a working switch? Does the data center staff need to get involved, or are you racking machines yourself? Are there enough rack screws? Power drill batteries? Crossover cables? How long is this entire process going to take?

6. OS/application/configuration installation

   In the next chapter, we'll talk about deployment scenarios that involve automatic OS installation, software deployment, and configuration management. However, just because it's automated doesn't mean it doesn't take time and that you shouldn't be aware of any problems that can arise.

7. Testing

   Do you have a QA team? Do you have a QA environment? Testing your application means having some process by which you can functionally test all the bits you need to make sure everything is in its right place. Entire books are written on this topic; I'll just remind you that it's a necessary step in the journey toward production life as a server.

8. Deploy your new equipment

   It's not over until the fat server sings. Putting a machine into production should be straightforward. When doing so, you should use the same process to measure the capacity of your new servers as outlined in the Chapter 3. Maybe you'll want to ramp up the production traffic the machine receives by increasing its weight in the load-balanced pool. If you know this new capacity relieves a bottleneck, you'll want to watch any effect that has on your traffic.

The Effects of Increasing Capacity

All of the segments within your infrastructure interact in various ways. Clients make requests to the web servers, which in turn make requests to databases, caching servers, storage, and all sorts of miscellaneous components. Layers of infrastructure work together to respond to users by providing web pages, pieces of web pages, or confirmations that they've performed some action, such as uploading a photo.

When one or more of those layers encounters a bottleneck, you bring your attention to bear, figure out how much more capacity you need, and then deploy it. Depending on how bottlenecked that layer or cluster is, you may find you'll see second-order effects of that new deployment, and end up simply moving the traffic jam to yet another part of your architecture.

For example, let's assume your website involves a web server and a database. One of the ways organizations can help scale their application is to cache computationally expensive database results. Deploying something like *memcached* can allow you to do this. In a nutshell, it means for certain database queries you choose, you can consult an in-memory cache before hitting the database. This is done primarily for the dual purpose of speeding up the query and reducing load on the database server for results that are frequently returned.

The most noticeable benefit is queries that used to take seconds to process might take as little as a few milliseconds, which means your web server will be able to send the response to the client more quickly. Ironically, there's a side effect to this; when users are not waiting for pages as long, they have a tendency to click on links faster, causing more load on the web servers. It's not uncommon to see *memcached* deployments turn into web server capacity issues rather quickly.

Long-Term Trends

Now you know how to apply the statistics collected in Chapter 3 to immediate needs. But you may also want to view your site from a more global perspective—both in the literal sense (as your site becomes popular internationally), and in a figurative sense, as you look at the issues surrounding the product and the site's strategy.

Traffic Pattern Changes

As mentioned earlier, getting to know the peaks and valleys of your various resources and application usage is paramount to predicting the future. As you gain more and more history with your metrics, you may be able to perceive more subtle trends that will inform your long-term decisions.

For example, let's take a look at Figure 4-15, which illustrates a typical traffic pattern for a web server.

Figure 4-15 shows a pretty typical U.S. daily traffic pattern. The load rises slowly in the morning, East Coast time, as users begin browsing. These users go to lunch as West Coast users come online, keeping up the load, which finally drops off as people leave work. At this point, the load drops to only those users browsing over night.

As your usage grows, you can expect this graph to grow vertically as more users visit your site during the same peaks and valleys. But if your audience grows more internationally, the bump you see every day will widen as the number of active user time zones increases. As seen in Figure 4-16, you may even see distinct bumps after the U.S. drop-off if your site's popularity grows in a region further away than Europe.

Figure 4-16 displays two daily traffic patterns, taken one year apart, and superimposed one on top of the other. What once was a smooth bump and decline has become a two-peak bump, due to the global effect of popularity.

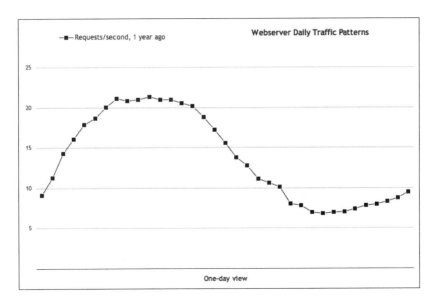

FIGURE 4-15. Typical daily web server traffic pattern

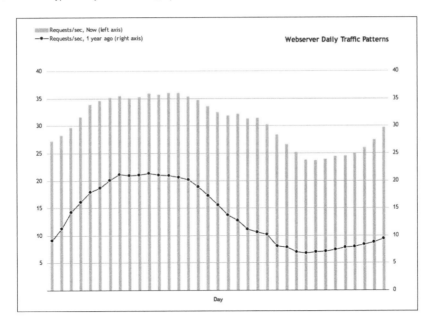

FIGURE 4-16. Daily traffic patterns grow wider with increasing international usage

Of course, your product and marketing people are probably very aware of the demographics and geographic distribution of your audience, but tying this data to your system's resources can help you predict your capacity needs.

Figure 4-16 also shows that your web servers must sustain their peak traffic for longer periods of time. This will indicate when you should schedule any maintenance windows to minimize the effect of downtime or degraded service to the users. Notice the ratio between your peak and your low period has changed as well. This will affect how many servers you can stand to lose to failure during those periods, which is effectively the ceiling of your cluster.

It's important to watch the change in your application's traffic pattern, not only for operational issues, but to drive capacity decisions, such as whether to deploy any capacity into international data centers.

FORECASTING CONSIDERATIONS FOR MULTIPLE DATA CENTERS

When your site's growth dictates serving content out of multiple data centers, you might notice certain geographic traffic patterns can emerge you may not have seen with a single data center. At the time of this writing, Flickr serves photos from eight different locations in the U.S., and will soon be serving photos from European and Asian locations as well. Our data centers in the U.S. are split between the east and west coasts, and users pull content from the data center to which they are geographically closest. Photos are distributed into what we term *photo farms*. A farm is made up of a mirrored pair of data centers, one on each coast. We currently have four farms (thus eight different data centers), with each farm containing a unique set of photos. We store each photo in the two locations for redundancy, in the event of emergency, or if one of a farm's data centers needs to be taken offline for maintenance.

When we first launched our second location, we noticed the east coast data center received as much as 65–70 percent more traffic at peak than its west coast counterpart. This was easily explained, as at the time our European users were a much more engaged audience than our Asian users, and since the U.S. east coast is closer to Europe, the usage was commensurately higher. In addition, we noticed the west coast data centers received considerably more requests for the larger, original sizes of photos than the east coast. We've attributed this to home broadband connections in Asia having higher bandwidth limits, so they're accustomed to downloading larger amounts of data. The usage gap has narrowed as the Asian user base has become more engaged, but overall activity is still higher in the east.

What this meant was our peaks and valleys differed for each side of each farm, and therefore our forecasts needed to be adjusted when we planned for growth. As just mentioned, the architecture for each data center in a farm dictates it must be able to handle 100 percent of the traffic for entire farm in the event its partner data center falls out of operation. Therefore, capacity forecasts need to be based on the cumulative peaks of both data centers in a farm.

As I alluded to in Chapter 3 ("Knowing Your Waves"), when you deploy capacity to multiple data centers, usage patterns can become more complex. You'll need to take that into consideration when forecasting capacity.

Application Usage Changes and Product Planning

A good capacity plan not only relies on system statistics such as peaks and valleys, but user behavior as well. How your users interact with your site is yet another valuable vein of data you should mine for information to help keep your crystal ball as clear as possible.

If you run an online community, you might have discussion boards in which users create new topics, make comments, and upload media such as video and photos. In addition to the previously discussed system-related metrics, such as storage consumption, video and photo processing CPU usage, and processing time, some other metrics you might want to track are:

- Discussion posts per minute
- Posts per day, per user
- Video uploads per day, per user
- Photo uploads per day, per user

Application usage is just another way of saying *user engagement*, to borrow a term from the product and marketing folks.

Recall back to our database-planning example. In that example, we found our database ceiling by measuring our hardware's resources (CPU, disk I/O, memory, and so on), relating them to the database's resources (queries per second, replication lag) and tying those ceilings to something we can measure from the user interaction perspective (how many photos per user are on each database).

This is where capacity planning and product management tie together. Using your system and application statistics histories, you can now predict with some (hopefully increasing) degree of accuracy what you'll need to meet future demand. But your history is only part of the picture. If your product team is planning new features, you can bet they'll affect your capacity plan in some way.

Historically, corporate culture has isolated product development from engineering. Product people develop ideas and plans for the product, while engineering develops and maintains the product once it's on the market. Both groups make forecasts for different ends, but the data used in those forecasts should tie together.

One of the best practices for a capacity planner is to develop an ongoing conversation with product management. Understanding the timeline for new features is critical to guaranteeing capacity needs don't interfere with product improvements. Having enough capacity is an engineering requirement, in the same way development time and resources are.

Iteration and Calibration

Producing forecasts by curve-fitting your system and application data isn't the end of your capacity planning. In order to make it accurate, you need to revisit your plan, re-fit the data, and adjust accordingly.

Ideally, you should have periodic reviews of your forecasts. You should check how your capacity is doing against your predictions on a weekly, or even daily, basis. If you know you're nearing capacity on one of your resources and are awaiting delivery of new hardware, you might keep a much closer eye on it. The important thing to remember is your plan is going to be accurate only if you consistently re-examine your trends and question your past predictions.

As an example, we can revisit our simple storage consumption data. We made a forecast based on data we gleaned for a 15-day period, from 7/26/05 to 8/09/05. We also discovered that on 8/30/2005 (roughly two weeks later), we expected to run out of space if we didn't deploy more storage. More accurately, we were slated to reach 20,446.81 GB of space, which would have exceeded our total available space is 20,480 GB.

How accurate was that prediction? Figure 4-17 shows what actually happened.

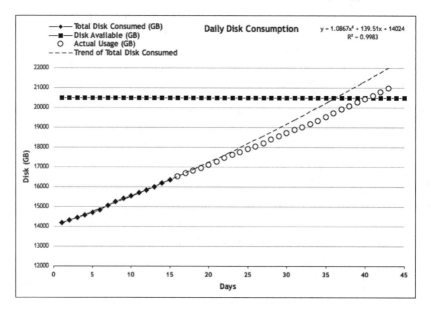

FIGURE 4-17. Disk consumption: predicted trend versus actual

As it turned out, we had a little more time than we thought—about four days more. We made a guess based on the trend at the time, which ended up being inaccurate but at least in favor of allowing more time to integrate new capacity. Sometimes, forecasts can either widen the window of time (as in this case) or tighten that window.

This is why the process of revisiting your forecasts is critical; it's the only way to adjust your capacity plan over time. Every time you update your capacity plan, you should go back and evaluate how your previous forecasts fared.

Since your curve-fitting and trending results tend to improve as you add more data points, you should have a moving window with which you make your forecasts. The width of that forecasting window will vary depending on how long your procurement process takes.

For example, if you know that it's going to take three months on average to order, install, and deploy capacity, then you'd want your forecast goal to be three months out, each time. As the months pass, you'll want to add the influence of most recent events to your past data and recalculate your predictions, as is illustrated in Figure 4-18.

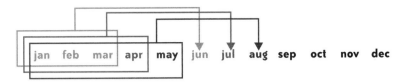

FIGURE 4-18. A moving window of forecasts

Best Guesses

This process of plotting, prediction, and iteration can provide a lot of confidence in how you manage your capacity. You'll have accumulated a lot of data about how your current infrastructure is performing, and how close each piece is to their respective ceilings, taking into account comfortable margins of safety. This confidence is important because the capacity planning process (as we've seen) is just as much about educated guessing and luck as it is about hard science and math. Hopefully, the iterations in your planning process will point out any flawed assumptions in the working data, but it should also be said the ceilings you're using could become flawed or obsolete over time as well.

Just as your ceilings can change depending on the hardware specifications of a server, so too can the actual metric you're assuming is your ceiling. For example, the defining metric of a database might be disk I/O, but after upgrading to a newer and faster disk subsystem, you might find the limiting factor isn't disk I/O anymore, but the single gigabit network card you're using. It bears mentioning that picking the right metric to follow can be difficult, as not all bottlenecks are obvious, and the metric you choose can change as the architecture and hardware limitations change.

During this process you might notice seasonal variations. College starts in the fall, so there might be increased usage as students browse your site for materials related to their studies (or just to avoid going to class). As another example, the holiday season in November and December almost always witness a bump in traffic, especially for sites involving retail sales. At Flickr, we see both of those seasonal effects.

Taking into account these seasonal or holiday variations should be yet another influence on how wide or narrow your forecasting window might be. Obviously, the more often you recalculate your forecast, the better prepared you'll be, and the sooner you'll notice variations you didn't expect.

Diagonal Scaling Opportunities

As I pointed out near the beginning of the chapter, predicting capacity requires two essential bits of information: your ceilings and your historical data. Your historical data is etched in stone. Your ceilings are not, since each ceiling you have is indicative of a particular hardware configuration. Performance tuning can hopefully change those ceilings for the better, but upgrading the hardware to newer and better technology is also an option.

As I mentioned at the beginning of the book, new technology (such as multicore processors) can dramatically change how much horsepower you can squeeze from a single server. The forecasting process shown in this chapter allows you to not only track where you're headed on a per-node basis, but also to think about which segments of the architecture you might possibly move to new hardware options.

As discussed, due to the random access patterns of Flickr's application, our database hardware is currently bound by the amount of disk I/O the servers can manage. Each database machine currently comprises six disks in a RAID10 configuration with 16 GB of RAM. A majority of that physical RAM is given to MySQL, and the rest is used for a filesystem cache to help with disk I/O. This is a hardware bottleneck that can be mitigated in a variety of ways, including at least:

- Spreading the load horizontally across many six-disk servers (current plan)
- Replacing each six-disk server with hardware containing more disk spindles
- Adding more physical RAM to assist both the filesystem and MySQL
- Using faster I/O options such as Solid-State Disks (SSDs)

Which of these options is most likely to help our capacity footprint? Unless we have to grow the number of nodes very quickly, we might not care right now. If we have accurate forecasts for how many servers we'll need in our current configuration, we're in a good place to evaluate the alternatives.

Another long-term option may be to take advantage of the bottlenecks we have on those machines. Since our disk-bound boxes are not using many CPU cycles, we could put those mostly idle CPUs to use for other tasks, making more efficient use of the hardware. We'll talk more about efficiency and virtualization in Appendix A.

Summary

Predicting capacity is an ongoing process that requires as much intuition as it does math to help you make accurate forecasts. Even simple web applications need to be attended, and some of this crystal ball work can be tedious. Automating as much of the process as you can will help you stay ahead of the procurement process. Taking the time to connect your metric collection systems to trending software, such as cfityk will prove to be invaluable as you develop a capacity plan that is easily adaptable. Ideally, you'll want some sort of a capacity dashboard that can be referred to at any point in time to inform purchasing, development, and operational decisions.

The overall process in making capacity forecasts is pretty simple:

1. Determine, measure, and graph your defining metric for each of your resources.

   Example: disk consumption

2. Apply the constraints you have for those resources.

   Example: total available disk space

3. Use trending analysis (curve fitting) to illustrate when your usage will exceed your constraint.

   Example: find the day you'll run out of disk space

CHAPTER FIVE

Deployment

ONCE YOU HAVE AN IDEA OF HOW MUCH CAPACITY YOU'LL NEED FOR FUTURE GROWTH AND HAVE PURCHASED the hardware, you'll need to physically install it and deploy it into production.

Historically, deployment has been viewed as a headache. Installing the operating system and application software, making sure all of the right settings are in place, and loading your website's data—all these tedious steps must be done in order to integrate new hardware that's fresh out of the crate. Fortunately, the pain of repeating these steps over and over has inspired an entire category of software: automated installation and configuration tools.*

Automated Deployment Philosophies

Although various automatic installation and configuration tools differ in their implementation and execution, most of them share the same design philosophy. Just as with monitoring and metric-collection tools, many of these concepts and designs originated in the

---

* A substantial part of this chapter was written by my colleague Kevin Murphy at Flickr.

high-performance computing (HPC) field. Because HPC and web operations have similarities in their infrastructure, the web operations community has adopted many of these tools and approaches.

Goal: Minimize Time to Provision New Capacity

The time needed to acquire, install, and provision new hardware must be factored into your calculations as you determine when you're going to run out of capacity. If your capacity will be exhausted in six weeks, and it takes you three weeks to add new hardware, you only have three weeks of breathing room. Automated deployment and configuration minimizes the time spent on the phase of the process over which you have the most control—integrating machines onto your network and beginning operations.

Goal: All Changes Happen in One Place

When making changes to hosts, it's preferable to have a central location from which to push changes appropriate to the servers you're affecting. Having a central location provides a "control tower" from which to manage all aspects of your infrastructure. Unlike server architectures, in which distributed resources help with horizontal scaling, centralized configuration and management environments yield several advantages:

- Version control can be used for all configurations: OS, application, or otherwise. RCS/CVS/Subversion and others are used to track the "who, what, when, and why" of each change to the infrastructure.

- Replication and backup of installation and configuration files is easier to manage.

- An aggregated configuration and management logging system is an ideal troubleshooting resource.

- This centralized management environment makes an ideal place to keep hardware inventory, particularly if you want to have different configuration settings for different hardware.

This is not to suggest that your configuration, installation, monitoring, and management setup should be kept on a single server. Each of these deployment components demands specific resources. Growth over time would simply overwhelm a single machine, rendering it a potential single point of failure. Separate these components from the rest of your infrastructure. Monitoring and metric collection can reside on one server; configuration management and log aggregation on another. See Figure 5-1 for an example of a typical installation, configuration, and management architecture.

Goal: Never Log In to an Individual Server (for Management)

Restrict logging into an individual server to troubleshooting or forensic work only. All configuration or management should be done from the centralized management servers. This keeps your production changes in an auditable and controlled environment.

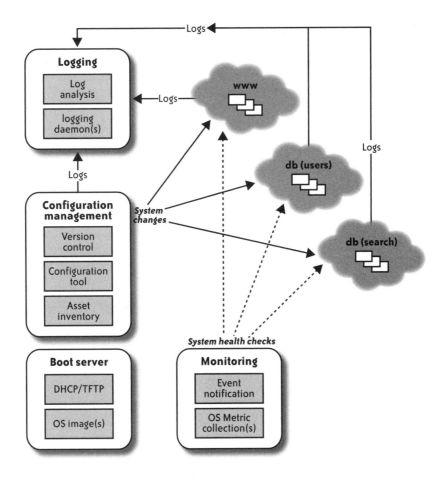

FIGURE 5-1. Typical cluster management scenario

Goal: Have New Servers Start Working Automatically

This is the holy grail of all deployment systems. You should be able to order hardware, add it to your inventory-management system, turn it on, have it automatically install all required software and register itself with your monitoring and trending systems, and then get down to work, all without administrator intervention.

Maintain Consistency for Easier Troubleshooting

Coordination of troubleshooting efforts during outages or emergencies is critical. Configuration management tools effectively enable that coordination. Consistent OS and software configuration across a cluster of identically deployed servers eliminates configuration inconsistencies as a source of problems. Troubleshooting in large production environments is difficult enough without needing to isolate configuration discrepancies between a handful of servers.

When tracking down a bug, the ability to quickly view all the changes that occurred between the last known good state and the present (bad) state can be invaluable. When more than one person is working on an issue, a centralized and consistent overview of all of the changes is crucial. With version control, changes are immediately apparent and tasks aren't repeated. Nor are they assumed to have been completed or otherwise mixed up with other tasks.

HOMOGENIZE HARDWARE TO HALT HEADACHES

In addition to making your software configurations consistent between servers that perform the same role, it's valuable to have consistency at the hardware level as well. At Flickr, we have two basic server types: a multiple-disk machine for I/O intensive tasks, and a single-disk machine for CPU-intensive jobs (for which most of the working set fits in memory). Limiting the number of hardware types has a number of advantages:

- It reduces variability between machines, which simplifies troubleshooting.

- It minimizes the number of different spare parts you need to keep on hand and facilitates cannibalizing dead machines for parts.

- It simplifies automated deployment and configuration because you don't need to create numerous special-case configurations for different hardware.

Virtualized infrastructures can take this a step further. You can buy racks of identical servers and allocate memory, CPU, and high-performance remote storage to virtual machines based on application need.

Automated Installation Tools

Before you can even begin to worry about configuration management, you need to get your servers to a state in which they can be configured. You want a system that can automatically (and repetitively) install your OS of choice. Many such systems have been developed over the years, all employing similar techniques.

There are two basic approaches to the task of imaging new machines. Most OS vendors offer a package-based installer option, which performs the normal installation process in a non-interactive fashion. It provides the installer with a configuration file that specifies the packages to be installed. Examples include Solaris Jumpstart, Red Hat Kickstart, and Debian FAI.

Many third-party products take a disk-image approach. A *gold client* image is prepared on one machine and replicated byte-for-byte onto newly imaged hosts. Often, a single image is used for every server in the infrastructure, with hosts only differing in the services that are configured and running. SystemImager is a product that uses this approach.

Each method has advantages. Package-based systems provide accountability; every file installed is guaranteed to belong to a package, and package management tools make it easy to quickly see what's installed. You can get the same result with disk image systems by installing only packaged files. The temptation to muck about with the gold client filesystem directly can lead to confusion down the road.

On the other hand, image-based systems tend to be faster to install. The installer merely has to create a filesystem and dump the image onto it, rather than download many packages, calculate dependencies, and install them one by one. Some products, such as SystemImager, even support parallel installs to multiple clients by streaming the disk images via multicast or BitTorrent.

Preparing the OS Image

Most organizations aren't happy with the operating system their vendor installs. Default OS installs are notoriously inappropriate for production environments because they are designed to run on as many different hardware platforms as possible. They usually contain packages you don't need and typically are missing those that you do. As a result, most companies create custom OS images suitable for their specific needs.

For a package-based system, the OS image is specified by preparing a configuration file that lists the set of packages to be installed. You can simply dump the package list from an existing server and tweak it as desired. Then you put the configuration file in the appropriate place on the boot server, and you're ready to go.

For an image-based system, it's slightly more involved. Normally, a server is set aside to be the gold client that provides the template for the deployed image. This can be a physical server set aside for the purpose, or even a virtual machine. You perform a normal OS installation and install all the software required in your infrastructure. The client image is then copied to the deployed server.

The Installation Process

If you're installing more than a handful of machines, installations with physical boot media such as CD-ROMs quickly become tedious and require someone to be physically present at the data center. You're going to want to set up a network boot server, which in the case of PC hardware usually means PXE (Figure 5-2), or Pre-boot Execution Environment.

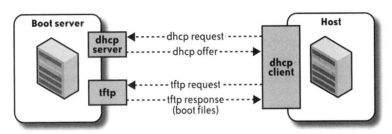

FIGURE 5-2. Basic steps of the PXE booting process

PXE-based installs are performed by a number of services working together. PXE firmware on the client requests its environment via DHCP. A DHCP server provides the information required to fetch the boot image (IP address, boot server, and image name). Finally, the client fetches the boot image from the boot server via TFTP.

For automated installation systems, the boot image consists of a kernel, plus a ramdisk containing the installer program. (This differs from diskless client setups, where the boot image contains the production kernel the client uses to mount a network volume as its root filesystem.)

The installer then determines what type of host is being installed and formats the local filesystems appropriately. There are several methods for mapping hardware profiles to hosts, typically they involve assigning configurations based on hostname or MAC address. For example, Kickstart passes the configuration file name as part of the DHCP options and fetches it from the TFTP server, while SystemImager has a configuration file stored on the image server that maps image types to hostnames.

The installer then installs the OS from the network onto the newly formatted volumes. As it pertains to a package-based installer, this means copying package files from a network repository (for example, apt or yum). For image-based systems, the OS image is dumped directly onto the local volumes, usually via rsync or a similar program.

Once the OS image is installed, the PXE server marks the host as installed. Typically, this is done by replacing the host's bootfile with a stub that instructs the host to boot from the local disk. The machine is restarted, and boots normally.

As shipped, most automated deployment systems require some manual configuration. DHCP server configurations need to be created, and hostnames mapped to roles. However, your inventory management system should have all the information about a machine required to boot it: MAC address, role, IP address, and hostname. With a bit of clever scripting, you can automatically generate the required configuration from your asset database.

Once this is set up, provisioning new servers is as simple as entering their details into inventory management, racking them, and powering them up. Reformatting a machine is as simple as assigning it a new role in the database and rebooting it. (Normally, a reinstall is required only if the disk layout changes. Otherwise, the server can simply be reconfigured.)

The deployment beast has been tamed.

Automated Configuration

Now that your machines are up on the network, it's time to configure them to do their jobs. Configuration management systems help with this task in the following ways:

- They let you organize your configuration files into useful subsystems, which you can combine in various ways to build production systems.

INVENTORY MANAGEMENT

Once your site grows beyond a handful of boxes, you will need a system to keep track of your hardware. Inventory management systems can be as simple as a spreadsheet or as elaborate as a full-blown web application backed by a database. These systems have a frustrating tendency to drift out of sync with reality as hardware is moved, decommissioned, or repurposed.

A way out of this trap is to make your inventory management system a part of your deployment infrastructure. By using information from your inventory management to direct your installs and configure deployments, you change it from a snapshot of your infrastructure as you *think* it is, to a source of truth that guides and instructs your systems.

One system to take this approach is iClassify. It supports automatic registration, as well as automated and manual classification. iClassify also integrates with Puppet for configuration management, and Capistrano for ad-hoc management of servers.

- They put all the information about your running systems in one place, from which it can easily be backed up or replicated to another site.
- They extract institutional knowledge out of your administrator's head and place it into a form that can be documented and reused.

A typical configuration management system consists of a server in which configurations are stored, and a client process, which runs on each host and requests a configuration from the server. In an infrastructure with automated deployment, the client is run as part of the initial install or immediately after the initial boot into the new OS.

After the initial configuration, a scheduled task on the client host periodically polls the server to see if any new configuration is available. Automating these checks ensures every machine in your infrastructure is always running the latest configuration.

Defining Roles and Services

You have a shiny new configuration management system installed. How do you actually use it? The best way to attack the problem is to divide and conquer. *Services* (collections of related software and configurations) are the atoms, and *roles* (the types of machines in your infrastructure) are the molecules. Once you have a robust set of services defined, it will be easy to shuffle existing services into alternative combinations to serve new roles or to split an existing role into more specialized configurations.

First, go through all of the machines in your infrastructure (or planned infrastructure) and identify the roles present. A role is a particular type of machine that performs a particular task. For a website, your list will include roles like "web server" and "database."

Next, go through each role and determine which services need to be present on each instance of the role for the instance to be able to do its job. A service in this sense is not just an OS-level program like "httpd." For example, the http server service would include not only the httpd package and its configuration, but also settings for any metrics, health checks, or associated software that runs on a machine serving web pages.

As you go through your roles, try to identify services that may be common to multiple roles. For example, every server is likely to require a remote login service such as sshd. By identifying these common services, you can create a single set of configuration routines that can be used over and over in roles you're deploying now, and in new ones that will emerge as your site grows.

An Example: Splitting Off Static Web Content

Suppose you have a cluster of four web servers. Each machine serves a combination of static content and dynamic pages generated by PHP. You have Apache's MaxClients setting tuned down to 80 simultaneous connections to ensure the machines don't overrun available memory and initiate swapping. The web server role might look similar to Figure 5-3.

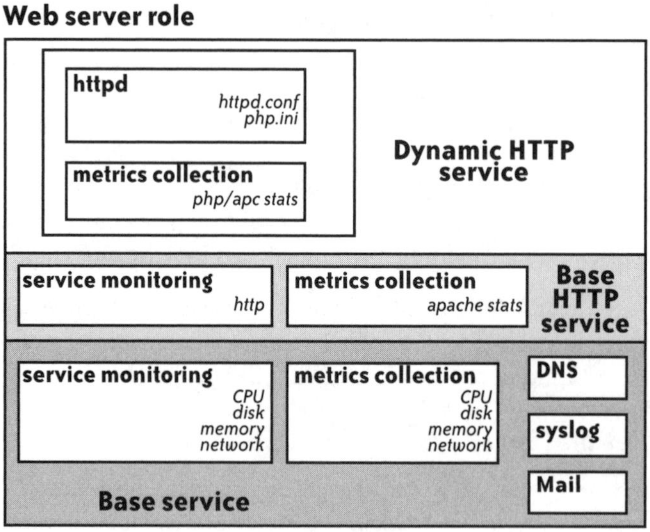

FIGURE 5-3. The web server role and associated services

You realize in a flash of insight that you could serve more simultaneous clients by splitting your cluster into two roles: one with the current configuration for dynamic content, and one with a stripped-down Apache with a larger MaxClients to serve only static content.

First, you split out services common to both roles into a separate service called base_http. This service includes settings that any web server should have, such as an HTTP health check and metrics pulled from Apache's status module.

Next, you create two new services. The dynamic http service contains your original Apache and PHP configurations. The static http service is configured with a simplified *httpd.conf* with a larger client cap and no PHP module.

You then define roles for each server type by combining these services. The new roles are depicted in Figure 5-4.

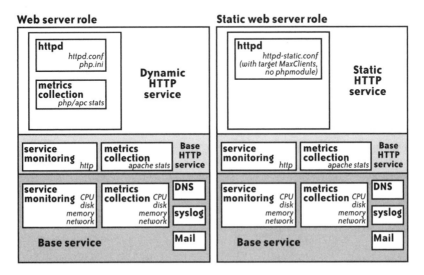

FIGURE 5-4. Static web server role and associated services

Now that the new role is defined, you can either go into your inventory management system and assign one or more existing web server machines to the static_webserver role, or deploy new hardware with the new role. If you decide to add more metrics or health-checks, which are applicable to both roles in the future, you can put them in the base_http service, and both roles will inherit them.

User Management and Access Control

User management and access control require special consideration. How do you control which users have access to which portions of your system?

In fact, there are several ways. Network-based authentication and authorization services such as LDAP are popular. Users and groups can be granted access to individual machines or host groups in one place. Permission and password changes are propagated automatically. On the downside, these systems represent yet another service that needs to be provisioned, monitored, and scaled as your infrastructure grows.

Alternately, it's possible to use your configuration management system to install user accounts on a host or role basis by defining services that make the appropriate changes to the system authentication databases. This is straightforward if you already have configuration management in place.

However, with such a system, password changes and access additions and revocations may not be applied to all servers simultaneously. Additionally, if automated configuration updates are broken on a host, that host may not receive the latest access configuration at all, which is an obvious security concern.

Both of these setups can be made to work. Which one is most appropriate for your infrastructure depends on your existing authentication systems, the number of users involved, and the frequency with which changes are made. If you are already using LDAP elsewhere in your organization, that may be the natural choice. If you have a small number of users and changes are infrequent, a package-based system may be appropriate.

Ad Hockery

So, you've achieved the dream of configuration management—an infrastructure full of properly configured servers that you never need to log into to manage.

But what if you want to? There are times when you may like to log into all of the members of a particular role and run a command. Fortunately, there are tools to make this task easier. These tools run the gamut from simple "run ssh in a for loop" scripts, to sophisticated remote scripting systems, like Capistrano.

Ideally, such a tool should integrate with your configuration management system. You want to be able to log into groups of servers by role, or even by service. This may require some scripting on your part to convert your role and service definitions into a format the tool understands. Alternately, the tool may be provided as a component of your configuration management or monitoring system (such as the gexec utility provided with Ganglia).

You can run commands on multiple servers. Should you?

In general, a good use for these utilities is to gather ad hoc data about your systems—perhaps information you're not measuring with your trending tools. They're also useful for debugging and forensics. The rule of thumb should be: If it's not something that you should be collecting as a metric, and it won't affect server state, it's OK.

When is it a bad idea? You should hesitate any time it would be more appropriate to use configuration management. There's always the possibility of forgetting ad hoc changes you made. You will regret forgetting.

Example 2: Multiple Data Centers

Eventually, you'll want to attack the greatest single point of failure of them all—the data center. You want to be able to continue to serve traffic even if your data center experiences a catastrophic power failure or other calamity. When you expand your infrastructure into multiple physical sites, you begin to realize the gains of automation on an even larger scale.

Bringing up another data center can look like a logistical nightmare on paper. It took you months or years to get your current systems in place. How will you be able to rebuild them in another location quickly? Automated deployment can make the prospect of bringing up an entire facility from bare metal much less daunting.

Rather than replicate each system in the original site on a host-by-host basis, the process unfolds as such:

- Set up management hosts in the new data center. The base installs may be manual, but the configuration is not—your management host configurations should be in configuration management as well!

- Tweak the base configurations to suit the new environment. For example, DNS configuration and routing information will differ.

- Allocate roles to the new machines on the boot server (or in inventory management).

- Boot the hosts and allow them to install and configure themselves.

To simplify synchronization of settings between data centers, it's best to keep all data center-specific configurations in a separate service or set of services. This allows you to attain maximum reuse out of your service definitions.

Summary

Knowing how much hardware you need does little good if you can't get that hardware into service quickly. Automating your infrastructure with tools like configuration management and automated installation, ensures your deployment processes are efficient and repeatable. Automation converts system administration tasks from one-off efforts into reusable building blocks.

Virtualization and Cloud Computing

TWO OF THE GOALS OF CAPACITY PLANNING ARE TO EMPLOY THE RESOURCES YOU HAVE ON HAND IN THE most efficient manner, and to predict future needs based on the patterns of current use. For those well-defined workloads, you can get pretty close to utilizing most of the hardware resources for each class of server you have, such as databases, web servers, and storage devices. Unfortunately, web application workloads are rarely (if ever) perfectly aligned with the available hardware resources.

In those circumstances, you end up with inefficiencies in your capacity. For example, if you know your database's specific ceiling (limit) is determined by its memory or disk usage, but meanwhile it uses very little CPU, then there's no reason to buy servers with two quad-core CPUs. That resource (and investment) will simply be wasted unless you direct the server to work on other CPU-intensive tasks. Even buying a single CPU may be overkill. But often, that's all that's available, so you end up with idle resources.

It's the continual need to balance correct resources to workload demand that makes capacity planning so important, and in recent years some technologies and approaches have emerged that render this balance easier to manage, with ever-finer granularity.

Server *virtualization* and *cloud computing* are two such approaches, and it's worth exploring what they mean in the context of capacity planning.

Virtualization

There are many definitions of virtualization. In general, virtualization is the abstraction of computing resources at various levels of a computer. Hardware, application, and operating system levels are some of the few places in which this abstraction can take place, but in the context of growing web operations, virtualization is generally used to describe OS abstraction, otherwise known as server virtualization.

An example of this is the Xen virtual machine monitor, or VMWare's ESX server, where a bottom-level OS functions with guest operating systems running on top of it. The bottom-level OS, known as the *hypervisor,* can be thought of as the brains of the virtualization. It allows the guest operating systems to share resources and easily be created, destroyed, or migrated to other hosts.

Entire books are written on the topic of virtualization. As it relates to capacity planning, virtualization allows for more granular control of how resources are used at the *bare metal* level. Figure A-1 illustrates this concept.

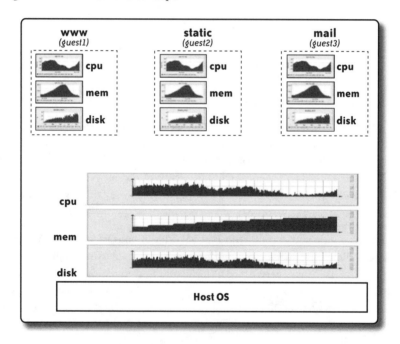

FIGURE A-1. *Virtual servers running on bare-metal hardware*

Figure A-1 shows multiple guest operating systems running on the same server. There are many advantages to employing this abstraction:

Efficient use of resources

There's no reason to waste an entire server to run small tasks like corporate email. If there are spare CPU, memory, or disk resources, you can pile on other services to that resource to make better use it. Because of this, organizations use virtualization to consolidate many servers to run on a single piece of hardware.

Portability and fault tolerance

When a physical host is reaching known (or perhaps unknown) limits, or suffers a hardware failure, a guest OS (and its associated load) can be safely migrated to another host.

Development sandboxes

Because entire operating systems can be created and destroyed without harming the underlying host environment, virtualization is ideal for building multiple development environments that demand different operating systems, kernels, or system configurations. If there's a major bug that causes the entire test-bed to explode, no problem—it can be easily recreated.

Less management overhead

Virtualization allows you to consolidate several individual servers with idle resources into fewer servers with higher resource utilization. This can translate into reduced power consumption, as well as a smaller data center footprint. Another benefit of less hardware is there are fewer parts subject to failure, such as disk drives, CPUs, and power supplies. Of course, the counterpoint to this is consolidation can increase your exposure to a single-point-of-failure (SPOF) as many services are dependent on the same physical hardware. Virtualization packages solve this potential problem by allowing virtual machines to easily migrate from server to server for disaster recovery, and for rebalancing workloads.

Virtualization essentially allows you to do more work with less hardware. These efficiencies have a tradeoff in that they can complicate measurements. Identifying which resource is virtual usage, and which is physical can be confusing, as the abstraction layer introduces another level of metric collection and measurement.

One additional advantage to virtualization is you can separate out application ceilings on a role-by-role basis, even when you are only running on a single physical server. For example, let's say you're consolidating email, backup, and logging services onto a single server. You may allocate more memory to the logging services for buffering the log writes to disk, and you may allocate more disk space to the backup application so it has room to grow.

As long as you can keep track of the virtual and the physical, the capacity planning process is roughly the same. Consider your physical servers as generic containers in which you can run a limited number of virtual servers.

Cloud Computing

The concept of packaging up computing resources (computation, storage) into rentable units, like power and telephone utilities, isn't a new one. Virtualization technologies have spawned an entire industry of computing "utility" providers, who leverage the efficiencies inherent in virtualization to build what are known as *clouds*. Cloud service providers then make those resources available on a cost-per-usage basis via an API, or other means. Since cloud computing and storage essentially takes some of the infrastructure deployment and management out of the hands of the developer, using cloud infrastructure can be an attractive alternative to running your own servers. But as with virtualization, you lose some of the ability to monitor and precisely measure your usage.

Computing Resource Evolutions

No matter how you look at it, your website needs computing and storage resources. Somewhere—whether in your direct and total control or not—a server will need to respond to client requests for data, and those requests may need some amount of computation and data retrieval.

Virtualization has been around almost as long as computing. At one time, computers were seen as equipment only managed by large financial, educational, or research institutions. Since computers were extremely expensive, IBM and other manufacturers built large-scale minicomputers and mainframes to handle processing for multiple users at once, utilizing many of the virtualization concepts still in use today. Users would be granted slices of computation time from mainframe machines, accessing them from *thin*, or *dumb*, terminals. Users submitted jobs whose computation contended for resources. The centralized system was managed via queues, virtual operating systems, and system accounting that governed resource allocation. All of the heavy lifting of computation was handled by the mainframe and its operators, and was largely invisible to the end users. The design of these systems was largely driven by security and reliability, so considerable effort was applied to containing user environments and data redundancy. Figure A-2 illustrates the client-sever structure in a mainframe environment.

Mixed Definitions

Grid computing, cloud computing and services, managed and virtual hosting, utility services: as with many emerging technologies, terminology can sometimes be confusing—especially when they become popular. The concept of cloud computing is not immune from appellation bewilderment. Vendors, marketers, consultants, and service providers stretch the term to include nearly any scenario wherein a generic and scalable infrastructure is made available to many users on a pay-per-resource basis.

Even the marketing for various cloud computing providers acknowledges this confusion. Some of the more broad categories for these are:

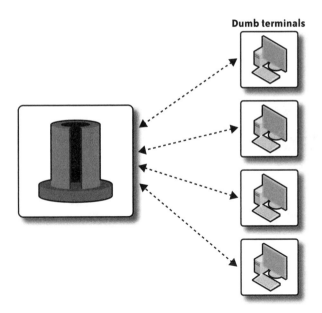

Dumb terminals

FIGURE A-2. Mainframe computing and the client-server paradigm

Cloud infrastructure

These are services such as Amazon Web Services and FlexiScale. They provide the lower-level elements that most resemble a managed hosting environment, with API access to control many of the services, including the ability to increase or decrease the capacity. Computation and storage are currently the main offerings.

Platform clouds

Google's AppEngine is an example of a service that, within certain constraints, allows customers to write code that runs in a specialized environment, abstracted away from the underlying operating system and hardware resources. Web applications have access to a non-relational database that will expand or contract as usage dictates, up to prescribed limits.

Application clouds

Salesforce.com's browser-based hosted applications are specific applications written by a vendor for specific purposes, and allow API access to applications built upon them. This is also known as SaaS, or "software-as-a-service."

For the most part, growing web applications have been looking to the first category for solutions to scaling their backend infrastructure, but as I said, this is an emerging and evolving technology. The levels of abstraction, development environments, and deployment constraints for each type of cloud computing will be right for some applications, but not for others.

There's been enough history in the cloud infrastructure category that a number of businesses have moved some of their mission-critical operations to this model with success. We'll look at some example cases a little later.

Cloud infrastructure is in many ways the next step in the evolution of the computing paradigm, which began with the mainframe. As shown in Figure A-3, cloud providers build, manage, and maintain all the physical hardware, organized in a virtualized cloud, while the customers of those computation and storage services can be both individuals and businesses.

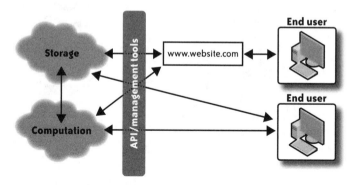

FIGURE A-3. Basic cloud infrastructure

The underlying architectures behind cloud computing is essentially virtualization expanded on a large scale. While there are varying types of cloud infrastructures, the prevailing variety are *compute instances* and *cloud storage*.

Compute instances are essentially virtual OS environments in which you can run your application's code. These instances can be built, torn down, and rebuilt at the customer's request. They may or may not have any persistent storage of their own to work with, so deleting an instance may wipe out the data you've written there.

On the other hand, cloud storage is basically a place to store data, and customers are billed a monthly usage rate along with transfer charges for reading and writing to the storage.

Farms of different classes of servers comprise each tier of cloud service, whether it be pure storage (in the case of a distributed file system), or a varying clusters of compute nodes that are built to house virtualized guest instances of the customer's operating system.

Cloud Capacity

One of the most touted advantages of the cloud-computing paradigm is the reduction of hardware deployment and installation times. Indeed, a server that takes as little as 20 minutes to deploy with your automated installation and configuration process may take a minute or less with a cloud service provider. As far as planning goes, cloud storage and compute instances should be viewed as just another type of resource at your disposal. Just like a single server, for each instance of cloud-based computing, you have some amount of:

- CPU

- RAM

- Disk (persistent or non-persistent)

- Network transfer (in and out)

Each cloud resource still has its ceilings and costs, just as with your existing infrastructure. In many ways, the capacity planning process is exactly the same:

- Measure what you have consumed already (number of instances, CPU, or storage)
- Find your ceilings (when do you need to launch/tear down a new instance?)
- Forecast based on past usage

Why make forecasts if your deployment timeline is a matter of minutes? For one, forecasting isn't solely about staying ahead of procurement and deployment timelines.

The promise of cloud computing is that you can increase capacity "on-demand" *easily*, not necessarily *automatically*. Since every instance is essentially a purchase, many cloud providers put the control of those instances in the hands of their customers, and deciding when to launch new instances (and how many) can be crucially important in the face of spiking traffic. An evolved operation that is using cloud computing might automate the process, but the automation should be tuned carefully to react not only to the load behavior of their website, but the load behavior of the cloud itself. We'll see an example of this "load feedback" capacity tuning a little later.

As with your own servers, cloud resources cost money. One important thing to remember is the costs of cloud computing can rise surprisingly fast if you don't pay attention. Tracking those costs will become important when you have the power to launch 100 instances at once.

Use it or lose it (your wallet)

There's also an additional variable with cloud infrastructure that you don't normally need to consider when deploying your own equipment: metered costs. CPU-driven cloud computing is based on the premise that you only use what you need, when you need it. Economically, it might not make sense to turn on CPU instances and simply let them run at anything less than peak capacity.

Most cloud infrastructure providers offer a "menu" of compute instance items, ranging from lower-powered CPU and memory platforms to large-scale, multi-core CPU systems with massive amounts of memory. These choices aren't as customizable as off-the-shelf systems you own yourself, so when you determine your needs you'll have to fit them into these more coarse-grained options. You may find many smaller-sized instances are preferable to having fewer large-sized ones, but each application is different. See Figure A-4 for an example of a cloud computing pricing menu.

As we talked about in Chapter 4, in the traditional sense of running your own hardware, the purchasing and approval process in an organization might take some time, as buying hardware is capital investment in the business. Since cloud infrastructure splits that concept into tiny chunks of investment here and there, does the approval process remain the same? Your systems administrator might not have had the authority to purchase 10 servers without approval from management. With cloud computing, does he have the authority to launch any number of instances that, over time, will equate to the same cost?

Amazon Elastic Compute Cloud (EC2) Instance Types
(NOTE: types and prices as of 7/6/2008)

Standard types

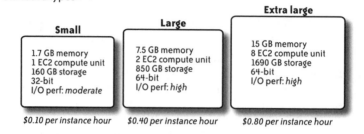

Small

1.7 GB memory
1 EC2 compute unit
160 GB storage
32-bit
I/O perf: *moderate*

$0.10 per instance hour

Large

7.5 GB memory
2 EC2 compute unit
850 GB storage
64-bit
I/O perf: *high*

$0.40 per instance hour

Extra large

15 GB memory
8 EC2 compute unit
1690 GB storage
64-bit
I/O perf: *high*

$0.80 per instance hour

High-CPU types

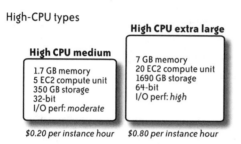

High CPU medium

1.7 GB memory
5 EC2 compute unit
350 GB storage
32-bit
I/O perf: *moderate*

$0.20 per instance hour

High CPU extra large

7 GB memory
20 EC2 compute unit
1690 GB storage
64-bit
I/O perf: *high*

$0.80 per instance hour

FIGURE A-4. Amazon EC2 menu: choices and prices

The point here is that tracking costs is another reason to pay attention and measure your cloud usage in the same way you would your own resources.

Measuring the clouds

When you operate your own infrastructure, you have many options for measuring your current capacity. Metric collection tools for historical data and trending, event monitoring for critical threshold altering, and of course OS-level tools for ad-hoc troubleshooting; these are among the tools we've talked about in this book.

Because cloud infrastructure is in many ways a "black box," and because most cloud service providers offer a relatively limited menu of resource choices, the importance of effective measurement becomes even clearer. Even though deployment timelines can shrink significantly with cloud services, you should still be paying attention to the rest of the capacity planning process. Finding your ceilings is still a necessity, and deploying new instances ahead of growth still follows that.

In the case of storage consumption, you can offload the forecasting to your cloud provider; it's their job to stay ahead of that curve. However, in the case of compute instances, the amount of actual "work" you'll get out of them is going to depend largely on the size/class of the instance, and your application's resource usage (taking into account, of course, the size/class of the instance).

Outside of the normal reasons for measuring your cloud's capacity, there are other reasons for setting metric collection and event notification in place:

- The performance of any of your instances and your storage may vary as the cloud provider shuffles capacity around to rebalance their architecture for increasing load.

- Even if your cloud provider has SLAs in place, knowing when your instances or storage has failed is obviously paramount. A good rule of thumb: trust, but verify on your own, that the infrastructure is available.

- The rapid deployment of new capacity can happen quickly, but not instantaneously. It's worth measuring how long it can take to launch a new instance.

- While cloud storage may be auto-scaling for disk consumption, there may not be any guarantees regarding how fast you can retrieve data from that storage. Just as in the disk I/O-bound database in Chapter 3, storage throughput can be a factor in your capacity, and should be measured. The same goes for "local" storage I/O that any of your compute nodes experiences.

With most cloud providers, you may not have any clarity on how your allocated instances run (or sometimes where). They may be running by themselves on brand new hardware. They may be sharing hardware resources alongside other virtualized instances that have their own fluctuating capacity needs. They may be located on a network switch whose usage is close to its limits. Your instances may or may not have consistent latency in storing or retrieving data from its persistent storage. You simply don't know any of the physical details under the covers of your cloud provider's interface.

This lack of transparency brings some advantages. It allows for the cloud provider to make unfettered changes to their operation (which can enable the rapid provisioning of new instances) and also relieves the customer of concerns about the nitty-gritty details involved in scaling the capacity. But it also means you don't have all the details you may wish, especially when you're accustomed to having every detail at your fingertips.

Cloud Case Studies

Should you use cloud services for your growing website? The short answer: "it depends." The longer answer is, cloud infrastructure, like every technology, has its pros and cons. On the one hand, ridding yourself of deployment and provisioning hassles may be benefit enough for you to switch to clouds. On the other hand, you give up some degree of control that you may be used to.

It's too early in the history of cloud computing, and the variety of offerings is too great to set up heuristics and formal guidelines for when to use it. Anecdotes and case studies, however, can help you decide whether you're in the right class of user and what factors to consider. As I mentioned earlier, some businesses have been able to migrate some of their mission-critical services to clouds with varying success. To illustrate this, I've included some cases below. In preparation for this book, I interviewed a number of organizations that have either direct experience using cloud infrastructure or have evaluated them as part of the process of building out new capacity.

Each one of these use cases highlights how drastically different the needs, concerns, and benefits can be for each organization when using cloud infrastructure.

Cloud Use Case: Anonymous Desktop Software Company

A well-established desktop software company investigated using cloud infrastructure to store and host digital media its users would process and upload from its product. Being a desktop software company, it didn't have a large online presence until this product was launched. Nor did it have the necessary operational staff to manage the clusters of servers needed to provide the hosting. The company considered using cloud infrastructure, hoping to offload some of the deployment and management overhead that comes with a 24/7 online product. It evaluated the idea at the technical and business levels, looking at the pros and cons.

In the end, the company decided to run their own infrastructure, for several reasons.

Lack of suitable SLAs

At the time, SLAs were only available in very limited terms with most of the established cloud service providers. Being relatively new to the online world, the company didn't have high confidence in trusting a third-party (even a well-known cloud provider) with the reliability and performance of its customer's data, so the lack of a comprehensive SLA played a significant role in their decision.

Legal concerns of user data

A concern was raised about who actually owns the user's data while it's being hosted on the cloud provider's servers. Did the cloud provider have any rights to the data since it was physically located on its servers? Were there restrictions put in place that respected national or international borders with regard to hosting? Legal issues involving user data, privacy, and reliability are always fraught with what-if scenarios, and also played a role in this particular company's decision.

Cost

As it was an already established business, it had the capital to host the data itself, so the economics of using cloud services were different from that of a startup. Once the company factored in what it would cost to operate its own data center with the forecasts of the online feature's adoption, it decided the investment was going to be worth it in the long-term, based on the cost histories of cloud providers at that point in time, as well as the company's own Total Cost of Ownership (TCO) calculations.

Control and confidence

Another main reason for the company not to use cloud infrastructure was a non-technical one. Developing it themselves allowed the company to have familiarity with what it was building. If the system failed, the company felt empowered to fix it in whatever manner necessary. It also didn't want to redesign its application in order to utilize the cloud resources via the APIs. Finally, the company felt more comfortable that it could move to the cloud sometime in the future, once the feature's usage patterns emerged.

Cloud Use Case: WordPress.com

WordPress.com hosts over 2 million blogs (as of this writing), and gets upward of 30 million pageviews a day. The company's servers are located in three different data centers which all replicate their data. For some time, this made uploading media (video, audio, photos) difficult for the user simply because the company didn't have a good handle on deploying new storage, so it looked into using Amazon's Simple Storage Service (S3) as a backup/data recovery solution.

As WordPress became familiar with the service, it started to use S3 for its primary storage. The reasoning behind using cloud storage was not economics; at the time of this writing, S3 costs are actually three to four times more than if it bought and managed its own storage. The advantage it was looking for was the ease of deployment and management. Not having to keep ahead of storage usage meant they could focus on the other parts of the infrastructure and site features. WordPress intended to use S3 essentially as a near-infinite storage bin.

Because Amazon Web Services (AWS) charges for transferring data in and out of its S3 cloud, WordPress reverse-proxy caches the content it takes out of S3 to its own servers (see Figure A-5).

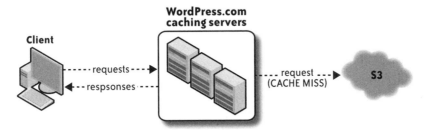

FIGURE A-5. WordPress.com reverse-proxy caching of Amazon of S3 storage

By caching frequently requested objects (or objects deemed to be "hot" enough to cache), WordPress uses S3 in the most efficient way possible, avoiding unnecessary transfer costs and serving content quickly via its own servers.

Caching in this manner allows it to use S3 as a near-infinite storage resource. It doesn't need to worry about the limits and overhead involved with incrementally deploying new storage itself.

Does this mean WordPress has ceased to do capacity planning? Far from it. It now has caching systems (and databases and web servers) that need to be scaled, but this is acceptable, as storage was its biggest pain point. WordPress was happy to redesign how it uses storage in order to avoid worrying about it again.

Cloud Use Case: Anonymous News Aggregation Site

An early-stage startup decided to use cloud infrastructure to run its development environment as well as its limited beta website. The site is designed to crawl the Web and index well-known news sources. The company would then process those documents with some natural-language algorithms in order to uncover articles in which its users would be interested. It used compute instances to do the crawling and would store both the raw data and the processed data in cloud storage.

While developing the site, the company noticed performance in its cloud-hosted application would vary, with no emerging pattern. Sometimes, it would bring up a new compute instance and notice the processing speed would vary from instance to instance, or would sometimes pause inexplicably in the middle of a computation.

In addition, since the company's processing was CPU intensive, it would launch many smaller instances from the cloud provider's menu of choices. As the application grew and the company started using more and more of the smaller instances, they considered upgrading to the next tier of the compute service for more CPU horsepower. While it was more attractive to launch fewer "large" CPU instances to have more processing power on hand, the pricing menu in place at the time made it prohibitively expensive when compared to the smaller instances. This meant it would be forced to continue running many small instances and accept the degraded memory and local I/O subsystems performance. This wasn't an ideal situation.

This gap in the cloud provider's pricing menu caused the startup to conclude it should run its own systems, and the organization began investigating managed hosting and co-location facilities. The cloud provider then introduced changes to its pricing menu, offering a "medium" level that better suited the startup's budget and capacity needs.

This case underscores that cloud infrastructure services are still evolving their businesses and still adjusting to their customer's needs with regard to configurations and management tools.

It also reinforces the importance of monitoring. When the startup began using Nagios to monitor its instances, it was able to see and record how the instances were performing, and make much more educated decisions on whether to launch more compute instances.

Cloud Use Case: SmugMug.com

SmugMug.com is a photo-sharing website, not unlike Flickr. It manages its own web servers and databases, but it uses Amazon's cloud infrastructure extensively for both storage (S3) and compute processing (EC2).

As of this writing, SmugMug.com used over 600 TB of space with Amazon's S3, and offloading this storage capacity to Amazon's cloud allows it to focus on developing new features. It started by using S3 as backup storage for its site. Once SmugMug felt comfortable with performance and reliability, it moved all primary storage to S3, even when Amazon Web Services did not have an SLA for this service (it does now). Moving storage was an easy decision for SmugMug because it saw economic benefits and also did not want to increase the size of its operations staff to manage in-house storage.

When photos are uploaded to SmugMug, they are placed in a queue that ships them off to EC2 for processing into their various sizes for use on its site as well as other photo processing actions. The same is done for uploaded video. Once the media has been processed, it's then stored directly to S3. This is an oversimplification of course, but during this process, SmugMug manages their cloud use in an interesting way.

Capacity feedback loops

Since SmugMug automates the transfer and processing of the videos and photos to the cloud via queues, it can control the rate at which processing jobs are sent, and how many compute instances it might need at any given time to handle the load. Every minute, SmugMug's system looks at a number of different metrics to decide whether to turn on or tear down compute instances, based on need. Some of the metrics it looks at are:

- Number of currently pending jobs
- Priority of pending jobs
- Type of jobs (photos, video, and so on)
- Complexity of the jobs (HD video versus 1 megapixel photo)
- Time sensitivity of pending jobs
- Current load on EC2 instances
- Average time per job
- Historical load and job performance
- Length of time it's currently taking to launch a new compute instance

By taking these metrics into account, SmugMug's system can appropriately scale up or down the number of EC2 instances it's using at any given time, thus making processing much more efficient than without cloud infrastructure.

SmugMug's use case follows the tenor of Chapters 3 and 4: marrying application and system metrics to plan for capacity, and making forecasts based on that historical data.

In SmugMug's case, it is aware of its ceilings, monitoring how close it is to reaching them, and adjusting its capacity on a tight, sliding window of time.

For SmugMug, taking into account its Total Cost of Ownership calculations, its desire to keep its team small, and its scale, it's economically advantageous for it to use cloud infrastructure for storage and processing.

Summary

Deploying your site to cloud infrastructure can change how you view deploying capacity, and largely depends on how you intend to make efficient use of it. In the use cases above, we see both non-technical, and technical considerations, as outlined in the lists that follow.

Non-technical considerations:

- Legal concerns surrounding privacy, security, and ownership of data by a third-party.
- Confidence in the availability and performance of cloud infrastructure.
- The effect of SLAs (or lack thereof) in the context of *pieces* of your infrastructure.
- Levels of comfort with a still-emerging technology platform.

Technical considerations:

- Redesigning their own application to make the most efficient use of cloud resources. Architectures that avoid transfer costs when possible and deploying compute instances only when you need them are very common practices.
- Not knowing where your data physically resides. This forces developers to think about their application (and the management of their application) at a higher-level. Expecting that compute instances can stall, disappear, or migrate requires redundancy to be built in.

Regardless of how organizations decide to use cloud infrastructure, its effect on capacity planning can be significant. Wordpress.com is paying *more* for their storage than it did prior to migrating its data storage, but is comfortable with that. SmugMug.com is paying *less* for Amazon S3 than it would if it were managing its own storage. Ultimately, there is no one-case-fits-all situation with respect to cloud infrastructure; each decision is dependent on the application and organization involved, just as with so many other technologies.

Clouds can shrink deployment timelines and provide more granular control over how you're using your capacity. These are facets of capacity management that we've discussed in the previous chapters, and should be applied to cloud infrastructure as well:

- Put capacity measurement into place—both metric collection and event notification systems—to collect and record systems and application statistics.
- Discover the current limits of your resources (utilization on compute nodes, for example) and determine how close you are to those limits.
- Use historical data not only to predict what you'll need, but to compare against what you will actually use.

Planning for growth using cloud infrastructure is an evolving area. Cloud providers have different restrictions, features, benefits, and drawbacks when compared to running your own infrastructure. But once you have a good capacity planning process, you'll be able to adapt your planning methods to take those into account.

Dealing with Instantaneous Growth

SOMETIMES EVENTS OCCUR OUTSIDE OF YOUR CONTROL, YOUR FORESIGHT, AND YOUR BUDGET. AN unexpected incident—technological or otherwise—can wipe out all your future projections. There are no magic theories or formulas to banish your capacity woes in these situations, but you may be able to lessen the pain.

Besides catastrophes—like a tornado destroying your data center—the biggest problem you're likely to face is too much traffic. Ironically, becoming more popular than you can handle could be the worst web operations nightmare you've ever experienced. You might be fortunate enough to have a popular piece of content that is the target of links from all over the planet, or launch a new, killer feature that draws more attention than you ever planned. This can be as exciting as having your name in lights, but you might not feel so fortunate at the time it's all happening.

From a capacity point of view, not much can be done instantaneously. If you're being hosted in a utility computing, or virtualized manner, it's possible to add capacity *relatively* quickly depending on how it will be used—but this approach has limits. Adding servers can only solve the "I need more servers" problem. It can't solve the harder architectural problems that can pop up when you least expect them.

At Flickr, we have found that edge-use cases arise (probably more often than routine capacity issues!) that tax the infrastructure in ways we hadn't expected. For example, some years ago we had a user who automated his webcam to take a photo of his backyard, upload it to Flickr, and tag it with the Unix timestamp every *minute* of every day. This makes for interesting database side effects, since we weren't expecting to have that many unique tags for so many photos. We've also seen users with very few photos but many *thousands* of tags on each one. Each one of these cases gave us insight as to where our limits existed, as we were forced to adapt to each one.

Mitigating Failure

The following tips and tricks are for worst-case scenarios, when other options for increasing capacity are exhausted, and substantially changing the infrastructure itself is impossible for the moment. It should be said this type of firefighting scenario is most of what capacity planning aims to avoid; yet sometimes it's simply unavoidable.

The following list of tips and tricks isn't meant to be exhaustive—just a few things that can help when the torrent of traffic comes and your servers are dying under load.

Disabling Heavy Features

One contingency is to disable some of the site's heavier features. Building in the ability to turn certain features on or off can help capacity and operations respond significantly, even in the absence of some massive traffic event. Having a quick, one-line configuration parameter in your application with values of *on* or *off* can be of enormous value, particularly when that feature is either the cause of a problem or contributing to unacceptable performance.

For example, the webservers at Flickr perform geographic (country) lookups based on client IP addresses for logged-out users in an effort to deduce their language preferences. It's an operation that enhances the user experience, but it is yet another function the application must handle. When we launched the localized Flickr in seven different languages, we had this feature turned on with the launch. It almost immediately placed too much load on the mechanisms that carried out the country lookups, so we simply turned it off until we could learn what the issue was. The problem turned out to be an artificial throttle placed on the rate of requests the geo server could handle, which was tuned too conservatively. We isolated and fixed the issue by lifting the throttle to a more acceptable level then turned the feature (which is mostly transparent) back on. Had we not implemented the quick on/off switch for that feature—had it been hardcoded within the application—it would have taken more time to troubleshoot, disable, and fix. During this time the site would have been in a degraded state, or possibily even down.

Ideally, you should work with the various products, development, design, and operations groups to identify an agreed upon set of features to which you can apply on/off switches. Currently, Flickr has 195 different parts that we can disable in the event of emergencies. These include photo uploads, all search functionality on the site, and more subtle features like sending "FlickrMail" between users.

When faced with a choice between having the full site go down, and operating it with a reduced set of features, it's sometimes easy to compromise.

A favorite story of mine is one I heard some years ago. A large news organization was serving web pages with the tallied results of the 1996 U.S. presidential election. Their web servers were running close to capacity all day. On the night of the election, traffic overwhelmed them. They had no spare servers to add quickly, and the website started crumbling, serving broken images, and some pages with images but no other content. The decision was quickly made to stop logging.

Now remember, this was before any large-scale traffic counting services were available, and all traffic metrics for ad serving were taken from the logs written by the origin servers themselves, audited alongside any ad-serving logs. By disabling logging, the site could continue and buy some time to assemble more equipment to handle the load. For hours, the site went without any concrete way to measure how much traffic it received, on what was certainly its busiest traffic day up until that point.

The decision to stop logging all traffic was the correct one. The relief on the disk systems was enough to allow the servers to recover and serve the rest of the traffic spike, which lasted into the early hours of the next day.

Baked Static Pages

Another technique frequently employed by sites hit with heavy and erratic traffic is to convert a dynamic page to a static HTML page. This can be either terribly difficult or very easy, depending on how dynamic the page is, but you can gain some safety by building static pages for only your most popular and least dynamic pages.

Converting pages from dynamic to static is called *baking* a web page. An example of how this can work well is using a news page showing recent photos that you update every two or three hours. Under normal conditions, the obvious design is to create a dynamic page that reads in the photos of the hour from a database or other content management system. Under duress, you could hardcode the image URLs into the page and change them manually as needed.

Baking your page into static HTML clearly breaks a lot of functionality found in today's more dynamic websites, but static pages come with some operational advantages:

- They don't instigate database lookups.
- They can be served very fast. Static content can display up to 10 times faster than dynamic pages that must wait for other backend services.
- They are easy to cache. If you need even more speed, static pages can be cached quite easily via reverse-proxy caching. This, of course, can introduce an entire new layer of complexity, but if you're already using caching for other parts of your site, it can be easily implemented.

The disadvantages of baking static HTML pages under duress are also worth noting:

- You need a framework in which to bake and rebake those pages quickly and easily. Ideally you should have a single command or button on a web page that will replace the original dynamic page with the static HTML replacement, and also reverse the operation. This takes some time and effort to develop.

- You need to track what is where, so when changes do happen, they can be propagated. The generation of the static content should be in sync with the content origin (usually a database). If changes are made to the database, those changes must be reflected (rebaked) to all of the static pages that include the content.

Cache But Serve Stale

Caching is used in many different components within backend infrastructures. Caching frequently requested objects from clients (or other backend server layers) can have a significantly positive effect on performance and scalability, but also requires careful deployment and increases the cost of management. Normally, caching done this way *accelerates* content coming from some origin server, and the *freshness* of each cached object is controlled and monitored by headers which can indicate the age of an object and how long it's desirable to serve the cached version of it.

As an extension to baking pages, and to take more advantage of caching, you can relax the content's freshness requirements. This is usually a lot easier than building static pages where there were none before, but it involves more complexities.

In times of trouble at Flickr, we've placed caches in front of our full-text search functionality in order to buy some time to isolate problems.

Handling Outages

When failure comes knocking at your door (and sadly, it will at some point), there are a number of steps you can take that can minimize the pain for users as well. Good customer service requires strong and effective communications between the operations and customer care groups, so users are promptly informed about site outage and problems, such as bugs, capacity, and performance. I thought I'd share some of the lessons we've learned when serving such a strong and vocal online community during emergencies or outages.

If your kitchen is flooded, but a plumber is underneath your sink, you at least have the feeling that someone has recognized the problem and is trying to resolve it. A good plumber will give you updates on the cause of the problem and what must be done to fix it.

Web applications are different: you can't see someone working on a problem, and users can sometimes feel left in the dark. Our experience at Fickr is users are much more forgiving of problems when you keep them in the information loop. We have forums in which users can report bugs and issues, and a blog (hosted outside our own data center so it can't be affected by outages there) where we provide updates on what's going on if the site is down.

An entire book can be written on the topic of customer care for online communities. Unfortunately, this isn't that book. But from a web operations perspective, site outages can—and do—happen. How you handle them is just as important as how long it takes to get back up and running.

Capacity Tools

MEASUREMENT, MONITORING, AND MANAGEMENT TOOLS INFORM AND GUIDE YOUR CAPACITY PLAN. IN THIS appendix, I've compiled a list of some of the more popular tools and utilities for your reference. We use a good deal of these tools at Flickr, and some of them are simply open-source equivalents of software that have been written within Yahoo! to achieve the same goal.

Monitoring

As we discussed in Chapter 3, there can be a lot of overlap in event notification software (tools that alert on resources based on thresholds) and metric collection and display tools. Some of the following tools have alerting abilities, some of them are more focused on graphing and collection, and some have both.

Metric Collection and Event Notification Systems

Ganglia, *http://ganglia.info*

    Born out of the HPC community, Ganglia has a very active community of users and developers. We use Ganglia extensively at Flickr, as do Wikipedia and other large-scale social networking sites.

Nagios, *http://nagios.org*
> We use a modified version of Nagios at Yahoo! to monitor services across thousands of machines.

Cacti, *http://cacti.net*

Zabbix, *http://zabbix.com*

Hyperic HQ, *http://hyperic.com*

Munin, *http://munin.projects.linpro.no/*

ZenOSS, *http://www.zenoss.com/*

OpenNMS, *http://opennms.org*

GroundWork, *http://www.groundworkopensource.com/*
> GroundWork is a hybrid of Nagios and Ganglia.

Monit, *http://www.tildeslash.com/monit*

Reconnoiter, *https://labs.omniti.com/trac/reconnoiter*
> Still in early development.

Ad Hoc Measurement and Graphing Tools

RRDTool, *http://oss.oetiker.ch/rrdtool/*
> Mature graphing and metric storage tool.

Collectd, *http://collectd.org/*
> Scalable system stats collection daemon. Uses multicast, like Ganglia.

Rrd2csv, *http://www.opennms.org/index.php?title=Rrd2csv*
> RRD to csv converter.

Dstat, *http://dag.wieers.com/home-made/dstat/*
> System statistics tool, modular.

GraphClick, *http://www.arizona-software.ch/graphclick/*
> Digitizer that constructs data from an image of a graph—handy when you have the image but not the raw data.

Deployment Tools

Automated OS Installation

SystemImager, *http://wiki.systemimager.org/*
> SystemImager comes from the HPC community and is used to install thousand-node computer clusters. Used by many large-scale web operations as well. Interesting work has been done to use bittorrent as the transfer mechanism.

FAI, *http://www.informatik.uni-koeln.de/fai*
> A Debian auto-installation tool with a healthy community.

KickStart, *http://fedoraproject.org/wiki/Anaconda/Kickstart/*

Cobbler, *http://cobbler.et.redhat.com*
> Cobbler is a relatively new project from RedHat, supporting RedHat, Fedora, and CentOs.

Configuration Management

Puppet, *http://reductivelabs.com/trac/puppet*
> Fast becoming a very popular configuration tool, Puppet has some very passionate developers and a very involved community of users. Written in Ruby.

Cfengine, *http://www.cfengine.org/*
> Written in C, it's been around for many years and has a large installed base and active community.

Bcfg2, *http://trac.mcs.anl.gov/projects/bcfg2*

Lcfg (Large-scale Unix configuration system), *http://www.lcfg.org/*

Cluster Management

Capistrano, *http://www.capify.org/*
> Written in Ruby, Capistrano is becoming popular in the Rails environments.

Dsh, *http://freshmeat.net/projects/dsh/*

Fabric, *http://savannah.nongnu.org/projects/fab*

Func, *https://fedorahosted.org/func/*
> Func is the Fedora Unified Network Controller, and can replace ad-hoc cluster-wide ssh commands with an authenticated client/server architecture.

XCat, *http://xcat.sourceforge.net/*

Inventory Management

iClassify, *https://wiki.hjksolutions.com/display/IC/Home*
> iClassify is a relatively new asset management system, which supports auto-registration and provides hooks for Puppet and Capistrano.

OCS Inventory NG, *http://www.ocsinventory-ng.org/*

Trend Analysis and Curve Fitting

Fityk, *http://www.unipress.waw.pl/fityk/*
> Excellent GUI and command-line curve fitting tool.

SciPy, *http://www.scipy.org*
> Scientific and analysis tools and libraries for Python, includes some curve-fitting routines.

R, *http://www.r-project.org*
> Statistical computing package, includes curve-fitting utilities.

Books on Queuing Theory and the Mathematics of Capacity Planning

Gunther, Neil. *Guerilla Capacity Planning* (Springer, 2006)

Menascé, Daniel A. and Virgilio A. F. Almeida. *Capacity Planning For Web Services: Metrics, Models, and Methods* (Prentice Hall, 2001)

Menascé, Daniel A. et al. *Performance By Design* (Prentice Hall, 2004)

Menascé, Daniel A. and Virgilio A. F. Almeida. *Scaling for E-business* (Prentice Hall, 2000)

INDEX

ceilings (*continued*)
    trend prediction requiring, 66
    for web server
        clusters, 86
        in load-balancing environment, 38
        for single machine, 39
Cfengine tool, 129
cfityk tool, 77–79
cloud computing, 108–113
    capacity of, 110–113
    case studies for
        desktop software company, 114
        news aggregation site, 116
        SmugMug.com, 116
        WordPress.com, 115
    costs of, 111
    measurements for, 112
    types of, 108
    whether to use, 113, 118
cloud infrastructure, 109
cloud storage, 110
cluster management tools, 129
Cobbler tool, 129
code examples, permission to use, xiv
coefficient of determination, 67, 68
Collectd tool, 128
compute instances, in cloud computing, 110
configuration
    access control, 101
    ad hoc, tools for, 102
    automated, 98–103
    consistency across servers, 95
    management tools for, 129
    roles, 99
    services, 99
    user management, 101
consumption rate of storage, 33–34
controlled load testing, 38
CPU usage, 36–38, 55–59
curve fitting, 66, 68, 77–79, 129

D

data centers, multiple
    deploying, 102
    predicting trends for, 86
data storage (see storage capacity
        measurements)
database
    capacity of, measuring, 40–45
    ceiling for, predicting when reached, 70–73
    failure of, determining load causing, 4, 18
    for metric collection systems, 25
    queries per second (QPS) handled by, 3
    scaling, 4
    slave databases, 4

Debian FAI, 96
demand, instantaneous growth of, 122–124
deployment, 83
    automated, goals of, 93–96
    configuration
        access control, 101
        ad hoc, tools for, 102
        automated, 98–103
        consistency across servers, 95
        management tools for, 129
        roles, 99
        services, 99
        user management, 101
    installation, automated, 96–98, 128
    tools for, 128–129
desktop software company, case study
        using, 114
determination, coefficient of, 67, 68
diagonal scaling, 20, 90
disaster recovery (DR), 22
disk usage (see storage capacity
        measurements)
DR (disaster recovery), 22
Dsh tool, 129
Dstat tool, 128

E

emergencies, handling, 124
event notification systems, 127
Excel
    macros in, for automating forecasts, 76
    trend lines in, 66

F

Fabric tool, 129
FAI tool, 128
failure of systems, predicting, 3
fityk tool, 77, 129
five-nines, availability measurement, 14
FlexiScale, 109
forecasting trends (see trends, predicting)
Func tool, 129

G

Ganglia tool, 25, 26, 28, 127
gold client image, 96
Gomez monitoring service, 12
Google AppEngine, 109
GraphClick tool, 128
graphing tools, 128
GroundWork tool, 128
growth in workload, instantaneous, 122–124

John Allspaw is currently the operations engineering manager at Flickr.com, the popular photo-sharing site. He has had extensive experience working with growing websites since 1999. These include online news magazines (Salon.com, InfoWorld.com, Macworld.com) and social networking sites that have experienced extreme growth (Friendster and Flickr).

During John's time at Friendster, traffic increased fivefold. He was responsible for Friendster's transition from a couple dozen servers in a failing data center to more than 400 machines across two data centers, and the complete redesign of the backing infrastructure. When he joined Flickr, it had 10 servers in a tiny data center in Vancouver; it is now located in multiple data centers across the U.S.

Prior to his web experience, John worked in modeling and simulation as a mechanical engineer performing car crash simulations for the NHTSA.

COLOPHON

The cover fonts are Akzidenz Grotesk and Orator. The text font is Adobe's Meridien; the heading font is ITC Bailey.

Related Titles from O'Reilly

Web Programming

ActionScript 3.0 Cookbook

ActionScript 3.0 Design Patterns

ActionScript for Flash MX: The Definitive Guide, *2nd Edition*

Advanced Rails

AIR for JavaScript Developer's Pocket Guide

Ajax Design Patterns

Ajax Hacks

Ajax on Rails

Ajax: The Definitive Guide

Building Scalable Web Sites

Designing Web Navigation

Dynamic HTML: The Definitive Reference, *3rd Edition*

Essential ActionScript 3.0

Essential PHP Security

Flash Hacks

Head First HTML with CSS & XHTML

Head Rush Ajax

High Performance Web Sites

HTTP: The Definitive Guide

JavaScript & DHTML Cookbook, *2nd Edition*

JavaScript Pocket Reference, *2nd Edition*

JavaScript: The Definitive Guide, *5th Edition*

Learning ActionScript 3.0

Learning PHP and MySQL, *2nd Edition*

PHP Cookbook, *2nd Edition*

PHP Hacks

PHP in a Nutshell

PHP Pocket Reference, *2nd Edition*

PHP Unit Pocket Guide

Programming ColdFusion MX, *2nd Edition*

Programming Flex 2

Programming PHP, *2nd Edition*

Programming Rails

Rails Cookbook

Upgrading to PHP 5

Web Database Applications with PHP and MySQL, *2nd Edition*

Web Scripting Power Tools

Web Site Cookbook

Webmaster in a Nutshell, *3rd Edition*

The O'Reilly
Advantage

Stay Current and Save Money

Order books online:
www.oreilly.com/store/order

**Questions about our
products or your order:**
order@oreilly.com

Join our email lists: Sign up
to get topic specific email
announcements or new
books, conferences, special
offers and technology news
elists.oreilly.com

**For book content
technical questions:**
booktech@oreilly.com

**To submit new book
proposals to our editors:**
proposals@oreilly.com

Contact us:
O'Reilly Media, Inc.
1005 Gravenstein Highway N.
Sebastopol, CA U.S.A. 95472
707-827-7000 or
800-998-9938
www.oreilly.com

Did you know that if you register
your O'Reilly books, you'll get
automatic notification and upgrade
discounts on new editions?

**And that's not all! Once you've registered
your books you can:**

» Win free books, T-shirts and O'Reilly Gear

» Get special offers available only to registered
O'Reilly customers

» Get free catalogs announcing all our new
titles (US and UK Only)

**Registering is easy! Just go to
www.oreilly.com/go/register**

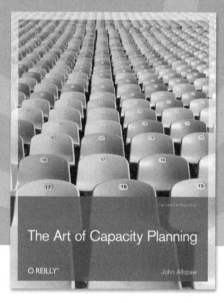